Wanderers

This book introduces the idea and experience of wandering, as reflected in cultural texts from popular songs to philosophical analysis, providing both a fascinating informal history and a necessary vantage point for understanding—in our era—the emergence of new wanderers.

Wanderers offers a fast-paced, wide-ranging, and compelling introduction to this significant and recurrent theme in literary history. David Brown Morris argues that wandering, as a primal and recurrent human experience, is basic to the understanding of certain literary texts. In turn, certain prominent literary and cultural texts (from *Paradise Lost* to pop songs, from Wordsworth to the blues, from the Wandering Jew to the film *Nomadland*) demonstrate how representations of wandering have changed across cultures, times, and genres. *Wanderers* provides an initial overview necessary to grasp the importance of wandering both as a perennial human experience and as a changing historical event, including contemporary forms such as homelessness and climate migration that make urgent claims upon us.

Wanderers takes you on a thoroughly enjoyable and informative stroll through a significant concept that will be of interest to those studying or researching literature, cultural studies, and philosophy.

David Brown Morris is a writer-scholar and Emeritus Professor of English at the University of Virginia, USA. He is very widely published, including two prize-winning books in eighteenth-century studies, and is internationally known for contributions in pain medicine. *The Culture of Pain* (1991) won a PEN prize and initiates a trilogy that includes *Illness and Culture in the Postmodern Age* (1998) and *Eros and Illness* (2017).

Routledge Focus on Literature

Trump and Autobiography
Corporate Culture, Political Rhetoric, and Interpretation
Nicholas K. Mohlmann

Biofictions
Literary and Visual Imagination in the Age of Biotechnology
Lejla Kucukalic

Neurocognitive Interpretations of Australian Literature
Criticism in the Age of Neuroawareness
Jean-François Vernay

Mapping the Origins of Figurative Language in Comparative Literature
Richard Trim

Metaphors of Mental Illness in Graphic Medicine
Sweetha Saji and Sathyaraj Venkatesan

Wanderers
Literature, Culture and the Open Road
David Brown Morris

Sham Ruins
A User's Guide
Brian Willems

The New Midlife Self-Writing
Emily O. Wittman

For more information about this series, please visit: www.routledge.com/Routledge-Focus-on-Literature/book-series/RFLT

Wanderers

Literature, Culture and the Open Road

David Brown Morris

LONDON AND NEW YORK

First published 2022
by Routledge
2 Park Square, Milton Park, Abingdon, Oxon OX14 4RN

and by Routledge
605 Third Avenue, New York, NY 10158

Routledge is an imprint of the Taylor & Francis Group, an informa business

British Library Cataloguing-in-Publication Data
A catalogue record for this book is available from the British Library

Library of Congress Cataloging-in-Publication Data
Names: Morris, David B., author.
Title: Wanderers : literature, culture and the open road /
David Brown Morris.
Description: Abingdon, Oxon ; New York : Routledge,
2022. | Series: Routledge focus on literature | Includes
bibliographical references and index.
Identifiers: LCCN 2021036311 (print) |
LCCN 2021036312 (ebook)
Subjects: LCSH: Nomads in literature. |
Nomads in popular culture.
Classification: LCC PN56.5.N66 M67 2022 (print) |
LCC PN56.5.N66 (ebook) |
DDC 809/.93352691—dc23/eng/20210930
LC record available at https://lccn.loc.gov/2021036311
LC ebook record available at https://lccn.loc.gov/2021036312

ISBN: 978-1-032-13683-7 (hbk)
ISBN: 978-1-032-18596-5 (pbk)
ISBN: 978-1-003-25530-7 (ebk)

DOI: 10.4324/9781003255307

Typeset in Times New Roman
by codeMantra

For Margot

Contents

Figures

Foreword

"*For months I followed strangers on the street,*" writes Sophie Calle in Suite Vénitienne (1983). "*For the pleasure of following them, not because they particularly interested me. I photographed them without their knowledge, took note of their movements, then finally lost sight of them and forgot them.*"[1] Calle follows one particular stranger all the way from Paris to Venice, not exactly wandering, but temporarily giving up control over her movements and even over her daily activities to carry out an arbitrary project—as writer, photographer, and post-conceptual artist—that has its origins in pure chance. Her life is temporarily not entirely her own but proceeds as if at the whim or will of the other. Her project consists less in actual wandering than in creating a simulation and documentation of what it is like—unattached from everyday roots—to *be* a wanderer.

Venice seems almost designed for the purpose of preventing visitors from knowing their way around. It is a city built to get lost in, where you cannot avoid the role of temporary wanderer, lost amid winding canals and alleys. Suite Vénitienne testifies to the transgressions and surrenders and letting go at the heart of wandering.

The guitar riff is my favorite moment in rock music. A riff is an improvised fragment. It is subordinate to the larger composition that contains it, and it also shifts what the music is doing—or about to do—in an altogether different direction, which provides a freedom otherwise constrained by the main theme or development. Truly memorable guitar riffs seem also inherently insubordinate. They tend to wander off, at liberty, as if the music were released briefly on its own recognizance.

Wandering can take the uncontainable, insubordinate, drifting, improvised quality of a dream. Not all dreams are sweet, some are nightmares, but dreaming regularly leaves the dreamer unclear about when the dreams begin, what they mean, and where they may ultimately lead after the dreaming concludes. We surrender to a dream state that we cannot control. It simply unfolds. Or, like the road, it unwinds. It offers a version of wandering in a patternless, fragmentary, improvisational drift that—no matter how short or long the duration—we apparently cannot help but follow, despite its tendencies to slip from brief euphoric freedoms toward states of idleness, loss, melancholy, or even exhaustion.

Sophie Calle on Day Ten: "*Alone, I wander back over the routes we took together these last two days, Henry B. and I.*" Day Twelve: "*Noon. I wander around Piazza San Marco.*" Day Thirteen: "*I wander listlessly along the streets. I'm weary. The afternoon slips away like this, forlornly, absent-mindedly.*"

Suppose that wandering—in its various hybrid modes and performances—proves basic not only to literary and cultural texts from Homer to Sophie Calle but also to acts of reading, writing, thinking, dreaming, and conscious self-understanding as we create ourselves, even absent-mindedly, as open, or secret, or unacknowledged wanderers. My main aim in the following 26 prose riffs is to begin such an endless unfolding.

Note

1 Sophie Calle, Suite Vénitienne (1983), trans. Dany Barash, Danny Hatfield, and Charles Penwarden (Los Angeles, CA: Siglio Press, 2015), n.p. The English "wander" accurately translates three different French expressions: "*Je parcours seule...*"; "*J'erre place Saint-Marc...*"; and "*Je déambule nonchalemment...*" (Sophie Calle, A suivre... [Paris: Actes Sud, 1998], 93, 98, 103]). On the somewhat complex history of its publication, see Rachel Taylor, "Sophie Calle, 'Venetian Suite,' 1980, 1996," Tate Gallery, April 2010, https://www.tate.org.uk/art/artworks/calle-venetian-suite-t13640.

1 Don't fence me in

I tramp a perpetual journey....

—Walt Whitman, Leaves of Grass (1855)

The mythical Wild West cowboy is a modest American gift to world culture and (not to be taken lightly) comes with a horse.

Henry James in his 1879 study of Nathaniel Hawthorne picks up on Hawthorne's famous lament about the things absent from American life and provides his own massive addendum:

> No sovereign, no court, no personal loyalty, no aristocracy, no church, no clergy, no army, no diplomatic service, no country gentlemen, no palaces, no castles, nor manors, nor old country-houses, nor parsonages, nor thatched cottages nor ivied ruins; no cathedrals, nor abbeys, nor little Norman churches; no great Universities nor public schools—no Oxford, nor Eton, nor Harrow; no literature, no novels, no museums, no pictures, no political society, no sporting class....

James continues his running list of national absences (so detrimental, in his telling, to the formation of an early American literature) until he finally concludes with a minor concession. "The American," he allows, "knows that a good deal remains; what it is that remains—that is his secret, his joke, as one may say."[1]

What is the redeeming American secret or joke? What specific feature did James see as offsetting the multiple absences in American life? It is the "national gift" of humor.

It is not surprising that James, cosmopolitan to the core, does not mention cowboys. He would take it for granted that fictional cowboy stories—which get their start in so-called penny dreadfuls and dime novels popular from the 1850s—do not count as literature. From a

DOI: 10.4324/9781003255307-1

literary point of view, cowboys are not serious, belonging to low-culture pulp magazines, and it would hardly impress James that Karl May (among the bestselling German novelists of all time) in 1875 introduces the fictional Apache warrior Winnetou in the debut novel of his immensely popular Winnetou Trilogy. If cowboys are too trivial to offer James even a token contribution to the hollowed-out national scene, it might be possible, in retrospect, to slip them in through the secret Jamesian loophole of humor. Few figures in American culture are more unwittingly self-parodic or joke worthy than the earnest, comical twentieth-century media confection known as the *singing cowboy.*

The singing cowboy has almost nothing in common with western ranch hands, who, in the tradition of the Mexican *vaquero,* ride horses, tend cattle, and mend fences. Their lives mostly disappear into the fictive stereotypes created by nineteenth-century urban writers in the northeast. Hollywood film westerns appear in the 1920s and help spawn the later 1950s cowboy series on television. Classic figures such as Hopalong Cassidy and the Cisco Kid—or the Lone Ranger and Tonto—ride on through changing genres and periods, but many of the popular figures are cowboys in name only. "Tex" Ritter (first name *Woodward*) attends Northwestern Law School. John Wayne, born Marion Morrison in Iowa, grows up in Southern California and attends USC on a football scholarship before the LA film industry transforms him into a laconic cowboy legend.

Wandering, as a byproduct of the wide-open spaces, is a distinctive attribute of westerns as a genre, but no figure does more to solidify the link among wranglers, wandering, and American culture than the once popular and weirdly fascinating cowboy who sings.

The singing cowboy, although manufactured by the film, radio, and recording industries starting in the 1930s, offered something that shoot-'em-up western heroes could not supply. It is not well known that, for example, John Wayne (before his monosyllabic stardom) was an early film singing cowboy, although he couldn't carry a tune and his songs were always dubbed.[2] Melodious, plaintive male voices invoking the lonely, wide-open spaces held a strong appeal to Americans feeling confined by the Great Depression. Radio listeners enjoyed the western harmonies as carrying an escapist, politics-free pleasure amid the anxieties of rising chaos abroad. The three all-time top 100 western songs—as voted in 2010 by the Western Writers of America—all appear in the early 1930s: "Home on the Range" (1933), "Don't Fence Me In" (1934), and "Tumbling Tumbleweeds" (1935).

Wandering is a recurrent motif in the favorite cowboy songs, helped along by mostly stay-at-home stars. Bing Crosby in 1933 first records

"Home on the Range." Two years later, "Tumbling Tumbleweeds" tumbles onto the scene in a 1935 film featuring one of the major singing cowboys and box-office draws, Gene Autry. Audiences didn't need to know that tumbleweed arrived in the west mixed with flax seed that immigrant Ukrainian farmers imported to South Dakota. Autry, whose résumé included a stint as an actual rodeo rider, offered all the truths listeners needed: tumbleweeds tumble and cowboys drift. Both affirm that a life of wandering is still possible, if only in a mythic *elsewhere*, while cowboy and tumbleweed merge into a single identity defined by its capacity to wander:

> See them tumbling down,
> Pledging their love to the ground!
> Lonely, but free, I'll be found,
> Drifting along with the tumbling tumbleweeds....[3]

"Tumbling Tumbleweeds," while instantly popular on radio, gained its greatest fame in audiovisual format when Autry performed it in the film *Tumbling Tumbleweeds* (1935). A generation before Guy Debord and the Situationists invented the concept of a wandering urban drift or *dérive*, Autry and Crosby help popularize the singing cowboy as a western icon of drift.

The singing cowboy in fancy western-style shirts (with pearl-headed snaps for buttons) adds an exotic glamour to the otherwise sweaty prospect of wandering through a land of sagebrush and heatstroke. The cowboy who strums his guitar by the campfire is no hobo but a figure straight out of central casting. His crucial accessories sometimes include a horse: as important as six-guns in representing male power, while also providing a sidekick to ease the occupational lonesomeness. A standard temptation scene offers the cowboy a chance to settle down and reject his drifting ways in order to marry the schoolmarm or heart-of-gold barmaid. The temptation, which means abandoning his horse and male freedom, must be refused:

> Cares of the past are behind,
> Nowhere to go, but I'll find,
> Just where the trail will wind,
> Drifting along with the tumbling tumbleweeds....

Wandering—aimless movement without a destination—is an antidote to confinement and takes the sinuous shape of the trail, winding and unwinding, with "nowhere to go."

"Tumbling Tumbleweeds" confirms the showbiz pedigree of the singing cowboy. It was a Canadian, Bob Nolan, who wrote the lyrics in LA, in between temporary jobs as a lifeguard and golf caddy. He recorded it with a vocal group called Sons of the Pioneers, which included the group's cofounder, Leonard Slye. Slye, a Midwest product, was a part-time actor who (in 1938) took the stage name Roy Rogers. Roy Rogers soon emerges as the quintessential singing cowboy at a moment when barbed wire, in use since the 1870s, was already converting the wide-open spaces into a patchwork of private ranches. Rogers helped keep the fantasy of western male drift alive well into the 1940s—long enough to launch one more singing cowboy classic, "Don't Fence Me In."

"Don't Fence Me In," although composed in 1934, doesn't achieve massive fame until Roy Rogers showcases it in a 1944 film alongside his sidekick-companion, the beautiful golden palomino Trigger. (The same film introduces him to future wife and costar, Dale Evans.) With its plea for "land, lots of land," the song crosses over from film to audio when Bing Crosby records it with the Andrews Sisters and sells a million copies.

Wandering in its singing cowboy version is usually a privilege of the white-hatted hero, but "Don't Fence Me In" adds a significant twist, as the lyrics are originally sung by an outlaw, Wildcat Kelly. The sheriff is sending Wildcat to jail. Jail, however, is no place for a free-spirited wanderer, even if temporarily afoul of the law, and the song conveys Wildcat's addresses to the sheriff:

> Oh, give me land, lots of land under starry skies above,
> Don't fence me in.
> Let me ride through the wide open country that I love,
> Don't fence me in.
> Let me be by myself in the evenin' breeze,
> Listen to the murmur of the cottonwood trees,
> Send me off forever but I ask you please,
> Don't fence me in.[4]

Wildcat, while a lawbreaker, has the soul of a Romantic poet, not least in ignoring the bourgeois zeal for real estate and lawful gain. Geologists are prospecting for oil, developers are selling vacant lots, and crime syndicates will soon transform Las Vegas into a resort for gamblers and postmodern French sociologists. "Don't Fence Me In," among its ironies, is the plea of a singing criminal whose purpose is to avoid confinement, meaning jail.

The singing cowboy and cowboy song, forgotten and almost comical, nonetheless help to situate wanderers and wandering as key cultural representatives enshrined not only in specific genres such as the western film or novel but also across much of Western culture. All well and good. But does anyone today know what a *Cayuse* is?

Cole Porter most likely didn't. He studied music in New Haven and Paris before residing in Manhattan, where he writes hit songs for Tin Pan Alley—the New York music publishing district named after the piano (*tin pan*). When Twentieth Century Fox asks him to write a cowboy song, Porter does what any city slicker might do. He buys a poem from a highway worker in Montana. He slightly reworks his $250 purchase, and the outcome is an overnight hit: "Don't Fence Me In." Attorneys from Montana arrive on cue to negotiate rights of co-authorship. Porter thus legally shares only one-half of the blame for a line that has surely puzzled singers ever since:

> Just turn me loose, let me straddle my old saddle
> Underneath the western skies.
> On my Cayuse, let me wander over yonder
> Till I see the mountains rise.

Cayuse preserves the internal rhyme with *loose*, following the internal rhyme-fest set off with *straddle* and *saddle*, not to mention the jingle *wander* and *yonder*. But what on earth is a Cayuse?

Readers of *Scribner's Monthly* in 1873 had a clear picture to draw on, even if they didn't know that Cayuse ponies (named for a Native American tribe) had a nasty disposition—as readers could hardly miss in the illustration (Figure 1.1).

The accompanying text continues:

> The ears are thrown back close to its head, the eyes put on a vicious expression, it froths at the mouth, seizes the bit with its teeth, tries to bite, and in every possible manner evinces the utmost enmity for its rider. Bucking is deemed as incurable as balking—whip and spur and kind treatment being alike in vain.

Not the horse a real cowboy might choose if he wanted a quiet ride home on the range.

Wandering is difficult for a person (especially a cowboy or an outlaw) who is fenced in. Wild animals in cages don't wander; they pace back and forth. *Yonder* indicates a vague general direction but not a clear destination or a specific route for getting there. As soon as you get there,

Figure 1.1 "A Bucking Cayuse" (1873). *Scribner's Monthly*, June 1873. Screenshot.

yonder has already moved somewhere else, forever shifting its location, always beckoning you to wander on. What is the best advice for singing cowboys or greenhorns as they prepare to wander over yonder? Think twice or maybe even three times before deciding to saddle up a Cayuse.

Notes

Epigraph. Walt Whitman, "Song of Myself," in Leaves of Grass (1855), ed. David S. Reynolds (New York: Oxford University Press, 2005), 39.

1 Henry James, "Hawthorne" (1879), in Literary Criticism, vol. 1 (New York: Library of America, 1984), 351–352.

2 See Stephen McVeigh, The American Western (Edinburgh: Edinburgh University Press, 2007); Richard A. Peterson, Creating Country Music: Fabricating Authenticity (Chicago: University of Chicago Press, 1997), 83–91; and Robert W. Phillips, Singing Cowboy Stars (Salt Lake City, UT: Gibbs-Smith, 1994).

3 Bob Nolan, "Tumbling Tumbleweeds" (1935), https://genius.com/The-sons-of-the-pioneers-tumbling-tumbleweeds-lyrics.

4 Cole Porter and Robert Fletcher, "Don't Fence Me In" (1934), https://genius.com/Cole-porter-dont-fence-me-in-lyrics.

2 Wanderers and walkers

Telegenic astronomer and astrophysicist Carl Sagan exhorts readers of Cosmos: A Personal Voyage (1980) to grasp and extend our heritage as wanderers. "We began as wanderers," he writes, "and we are wanderers still. We have lingered long enough on the shores of the cosmic ocean. We are ready at last to set sail for the stars."[1] Wandering is important less because it portends future space travel than because displaced and desperate climate migrants are already on the move as our planet heats up. Melting ice caps, rising sea levels, failing states, disappearing jobs, and killer superstorms are everyday news. We are all compatriots of the new wanderers, whether or not we know it.

Imagine the classic wanderer, with no plan and no destination. Such wanderers seem able to loosen controls, embrace chance, welcome contingences, and improvise. They can wander in the countryside or in a department store. A few classic wanderers achieve the status of archetypes. Most are everyday people belonging to a subculture of refugees, retirees, rebels, homeless veterans, gig workers, gypsies, drifters, artists, dropouts, or single mothers with children, to name a few. What they experience—as long as the road unwinds—is an imperfect freedom from the routines and mentalities of sedentary life: the condition of being footloose.

I've always been a *secret* wanderer. Somewhere along the way I must have lost the path, if there *was* a path. For decades I kept my wandering under wraps, hidden even from myself, and I had no clue that it was even possible to wander secretly. My admission finally came as I was hauling books to the recycle bin. Book lovers are no doubt shuddering in horror, and I was horrified too, which led to my moment of self-revelation. The new owner would take possession of my apartment in 12 hours. There was no time to find a good home for my books—old friends and the survivors of multiple moves—so I tried not to think about what I was doing as the clock ticked down.

DOI: 10.4324/9781003255307-2

Wanderers, if they are born wanderers, tend to have a restless spirit. I'm not restless, but my late wife was. She informed me sweetly early on that every few years she changed her job or her man. I knew my own self-interest well enough to encourage her changes in employment. We moved a lot. I came to wandering secondhand, a secret wanderer in love with a born wanderer.

Wanderers hear an inner voice that says *move on*. My inner voice whispered *stay put*, but, clearly, I just couldn't manage it. With my furniture sold, the cable box returned, and my prized engravings of *A Rake's Progress* donated to the art museum, I made a final trip to the dumpster in near darkness. Bone-weary, I finally had to admit that, yes, I am now a self-confessed, no-longer-secret, hit-the-road, footloose, terrestrial wanderer.

Are there other secret wanderers out there? Hobos riding the rails used a code of hieroglyphs: visual clues to indicate dangerous neighborhoods, the house of a kind lady, or where to find a meal.[2] I'd like to find some hieroglyphs. "I really have no anxiety about controlling my own life," says singer-songwriter-actor Kris Kristofferson at 80, a notorious wanderer, who wrote the classic wandering anthem about two hitchhiking drifters, "Me and Bobby McGee" (1969). "Somehow," he says of his long and wandering life, "I just slipped into it and it's worked."[3]

Unlike Kristofferson, I never thought of myself as a wanderer, but what exactly is it that I finally understand I've slipped into? We all wander from time to time. Young professionals in the US, burned out but flush with cash after a yearslong pandemic shutdown, are quitting nine-to-five jobs for unstructured, improvised lives.[4] Wandering, in their case, embodies a life choice or perhaps the shrug of a nothing-to-lose gambler rolling the dice. I suspect there are obsessive wanderers. Wandering, whether open and obsessive or secret and casual, entails a psychology of uncontrol in which, like Kristofferson or Bobby McGee, wanderers enter a mental zone of contingencies and planlessness.

Wandering enfolds us all—drifters or homebodies—in its rich cultural history. We all have a stake in understanding what remains a spectacularly underappreciated and understudied form of human behavior, especially in contrast to its alter ego, walking.

Walking has generated a surplus of appreciative, wide-ranging, even scholarly works, including Thoreau's extended essay "Walking" (1862), Colin Fletcher's bestseller The Complete Walker (1968), and Rebecca Solnit's semi-autobiographical tour-de-force subtitled A History of Walking (2000).[5] Duncan Minshull has edited three companionate books that collect reflections on walking by various writers.[6] Kinesiologists and nutritionists meanwhile cite the statistics to demonstrate that walking is good for our health, even if we miss the prized 10,000 daily steps. No one, however, seeks to demonstrate that wandering is good for our health. In fact, wandering has a bad reputation. Wanderers are unfocused, drifting, frivolous daydreamers. The popular mantra *be here now* suggests that wanderers aren't fully *in being*. Wandering dropouts from the ethic of mindfulness leave it dangerously unclear where, or even who, they *are*.

Wandering, especially in light of our long biological history as bipedal walkers, ranks among the more trivial human activities: an ordinary, nonserious, quasi-autonomic practice that arouses almost zero curiosity. A practice so easy to overlook may be more fundamental than we suspect, like breathing and sleeping. We may take it for granted, but its complete absence matters. In truth, miniature acts of wandering fill our days. Like daydreams, they pass unnoticed as we seamlessly return to weighty affairs.

What, then, is the difference between wandering and walking? Wanderers regularly walk, but relatively few walkers wander, so the two actions are not identical. Dictionary shortcuts don't help. We talk about wandering without stopping to define it. Everyone knows intuitively how to define walking—it's just what we *do*—an act we engage in, intuitively, as soon as we graduate from crawling. Wandering isn't intuitive. No one graduates into wandering, and its contrasts with walking prove instructive.

Walkers tend to have a destination and a purpose, even if just a walk around the block. Purposeless motion—crossing a room or crossing an ocean—sooner or later turns into wandering. Purpose and destination also endow walking with a value that wandering lacks: walking *accomplishes* something. It brings an action to completion, such as walking the dog. Wandering, by contrast, looks like a waste of time. It not only accomplishes nothing but also squanders energy: a resource that busy people (people of business) would put to better use. In this wastefulness, wandering actually accomplishes—this is hard to do—even *less than nothing*. Wandering, unlike walking, has minus use value.

Historical linguistics, oddly, can help where dictionaries fall short. Long before anyone spoke English, the words *wander* and *walk* had their origin in different Proto-Indo-European roots: *walking* refers to gait (coordinated bodily movements) while *wandering* refers to spatial patterns and sinuous shapes (weaving, winding, curving). Even today, wandering implies a spatial pattern of twists and turns, as in its synonym *meandering*, which takes its name from the river Maeander, famous for its winding course. (The technical description of winding watercourses is called *meander geometry*.) Historical linguistics doesn't determine modern usage, but it illuminates differences still in play. Walking usually refers to gait—what we do as pedestrians with our feet and bodies—while wandering refers to aimless patterns or patternless configurations opposed to anything like a straight line. Much follows from these basic differences.

Wandering as a movement through curved space has a distinctive relation to time and to transport. Walkers regularly keep track of time: they wear watches, keep promises, run errands, and come home at night, while wanderers have time to burn. Walking, as a pedestrian act, restricts the available means of transport. It requires legs and feet, actual or prosthetic. In contrast, you can wander on foot, in a car, aboard a plane, via wheelchair, or (like Captain America in the film *Easy Rider* [1969]) astride a Harley-Davidson with ape hanger handlebars. If there are 50 ways to leave your lover, as singer-songwriter Paul Simon counts them, number 51 (after *Hop on the bus, Gus*) is just to wander off. Our ancestor *Homo erectus*—finally standing upright after all those millennia—walked out of Africa on two feet, and two feet are mostly what walkers (who are not also acrobats) use today.

Homo erectus didn't just walk out of Africa but wandered. Alfred North Whitehead, whose "process philosophy" is increasingly relevant today, agrees. "One main factor in the upward trend of animal life," he wrote in 1925, "has been the power of wandering."[7]

Wandering and walking, while they certainly overlap in wanderers who walk and in walkers who wander, describe fundamentally dissimilar activities that extend to distinctive states of being. Wandering implies an aversion to straight lines. Walkers, with an affection for shortcuts, often choose a direct path, whereas wanderers tend to dither, if only because they don't know where they are headed. Any plan is provisional and likely short-lived. Odysseus sets out from Troy with the intention to sail home to Ithaca, but his plan goes badly awry, and he wanders for ten years. Linear progress from start to finish—the two-dimensional standard geometry of walking—proves antithetical to wandering. Wandering involves three dimensions and a compass that regularly goes haywire.

Wanderers don't necessarily seek out pathless spaces, like Huck Finn lighting out for the Indian Territory, but wherever a beaten path opens up they tend to go sideways. Straight paths and settled plans represent the road not taken, or what wandering *isn't*.

A final preliminary distinction: wandering differs from walking in its attraction to error. *Errare* in Latin means "to wander," and *error* in English regularly contains implications of wandering, with a whiff of blame, moral or legal: falling, offending, sinning, straying, trespassing, or transgressing. The notorious *wandering eye*—once primarily a male condition—suggests a tendency to go astray, whereas walking seems morally neutral, or at least seldom two-faced. Wandering, in its affinity for erotic adventures, not only leads toward trouble but also reflects the surrender of control typical of romance, when we give ourselves over to an unfolding impulse, blind to the future. "I love ignorance of the future," says the semi-autobiographical persona whom Nietzsche calls *the Wanderer*, "and do not want to perish of impatience and premature tasting of things promised."[8]

"**Lust now, wander later.**" So reads the boldface headline on a popular lifestyle website. The link, since disappeared, is clickbait meant to catch the surfing eye with its canny equation between wandering and sex: "Wanderlust. It's part feeling, part craving—a deep yearning to see, taste, touch a place far from home. Being grounded for now leaves ample time to daydream and plan for later. Slicing into a ripe Amalfi lemon, strolling through the Jardin Majorelle in Marrakech, hitting the farm-to-table circuit in Sydney…." Sex sells, as everyone knows, but it appears that wandering too *sells*. Is wandering itself now sexy? An online Wanderlust Shop pops up. Wanderlust demands the right accessories: a $515 Joseph dress, $295 incense set, $300 sandals. The space tourism market is even now heating up for billionaire wanderers with the surplus cash to buy seats aboard the *New Shepard*—its "massive windows" designed to offer space tourists an "unparalleled" view.[9] Perhaps even a certificate on splashdown.

Wandering, as I began to shed my status as a secret wanderer, quickly took on a fascinating literary and cultural richness. Traces of wanderers and wandering seemed left like footprints in poems and diaries, films and music, memoirs and histories, music and philosophy, even in television miniseries and popular songs. Prototypes and archetypes emerged, human and inhuman, fictive and actual. Meanwhile, who could not notice the heartbreaking scenes of migrants on the move, children jammed into detention centers, refugees in tent cities, rising violence against wandering strangers? It seems high time, if there are other secret wanderers afoot, to think openly and collectively about what it might mean—past, present, and future—to wander.

Notes

1 Carl Sagan, Cosmos: A Personal Voyage (1980; rpt. New York: Random House, 2013), 206. His subsequent book, Pale Blue Dot: A Vision of the Human Future in Space (New York: Random House, 1994), begins with a foreword entitled "Wanderers: An Introduction" (xiii–xxi).

2 Alan Marshall, "The Hobo Code: An Introduction to the Hieroglyphic Language of Early 1900s Train-Hoppers," *Open Culture*, 22 August 2018, https://www.openculture.com/2018/08/hobo-code-introduction-hieroglyphic-language-early-1900s-train-hoppers.html.

3 Quoted in Neil Strauss, "Kris Kristofferson: An Outlaw at 80," *Rolling Stone*, 6 June 2016, https://www.rollingstone.com/feature/kris-kristofferson-an-outlaw-at-80-183141/.

4 Kevin Roose, "Welcome to the YOLO Economy," *New York Times*, 21 April 2021, https://www.nytimes.com/2021/04/21/technology/welcome-to-the-yolo-economy.html.

5 Henry David Thoreau, "Walking" (1862), in Excursions, ed. Joseph J. Moldenhauer (Princeton: Princeton University Press, 2007); Colin Fletcher, The Complete Walker: The Joys and Techniques of Hiking and Backpacking (New York: Knopf, 1968), now in a 4th edition (2002) with co-author Chip Rawlins; and Rebecca Solnit, Wanderlust: A History of Walking (New York: Viking Penguin, 2000). See also, cited again later, Sarah Jane Cervenak, Wandering: Philosophical Performances of Racial and Sexual Freedom (Durham, NC: Duke University Press, 2014); and Matthew Beaumont, The Walker: On Finding and Losing Yourself in the Modern City (London: Verso, 2020).

6 See The Vintage Book of Walking, ed. Duncan Minshull (London: Random House, 2000)—republished as While Wandering: A Walking Companion, ed. Duncan Minshull (New York: Random House, 2014); Beneath My Feet: Writers on Walking, ed. Duncan Minshull (Mirefoot: Notting Hill Editions, 2018); and Sauntering: Writers Walk Europe, ed. Duncan Minshull (Mirefoot: Notting Hill Editions, 2021).

7 Alfred North Whitehead, Science and the Modern World (1925; rpt. New York: Free Press, 1967), 207.

8 Friedrich Nietzsche, The Gay Science (1882), ed. Bernard Williams, trans. Josefine Nauckhoff and Adrian Del Caro (Cambridge: Cambridge University Press, 2001), 162 (§287). Nietzsche published a second edition in 1887.

9 Alex Hern, "Jeff Bezos To Go into Space on First Crewed Flight of New Shepard Rocket," *The Guardian*, 7 June 2021, https://www.theguardian.com/technology/2021/jun/07/jeff-bezos-to-go-into-space-on-first-crewed-flight-of-new-shepard-rocket.

3 The happy wanderer

Wanderers (2014)—a remarkable four-minute film created by Swedish digital artist and animator Erik Wernquist—pans across stunning extraterrestrial scenes photographed by robotic spacecraft, supplemented or enhanced with computer graphics. A voice-over simultaneously records Carl Sagan reading his passage from Cosmos describing us as "wanderers still" and "ready at last to set sail for the stars." Sagan did not live to see Wernquist's film, but I wonder if it would have changed his mind. The film's stunning images strike me as a panorama of bleak otherworldly desolation. No springs, no lakes, no trees, no birds, no daffodils, no high blue skies with an occasional cloud drifting by. No moon over Miami. Fossil fuels and greenhouse gases may ultimately force us to wander for light-years in search of an uncontaminated planet or a planet hosted by tolerant space aliens, but first I want to know more about wandering.

An improbable pop song transfixed American radio listeners in 1954. "The Happy Wanderer" ranked 17th on *Billboard* magazine's annual list of top 30 singles, and its hyper-cheerfulness suggests that Americans in the mid-1950s needed more than a fantasy hike in the mountains, since they were willing to settle for sheer nonsense:

> I love to go a-wandering,
> Along the mountain track,
> And as I go, I love to sing,
> My knapsack on my back.

A musical fantasy at least offered a break from the imminent threat of nuclear war, as American schoolchildren scrambled under their desks during air-raid drills. In England, where "The Happy Wanderer" spent half of 1954 high on the pop charts, people also needed a shot of optimism or escapist fantasy in the aftermath of World War II and 14 long, hungry years of food rationing.

DOI: 10.4324/9781003255307-3

The international collaboration required to launch "The Happy Wanderer" rivaled the founding of the UN, in 1945, and the song (leaping over recent hostilities) took its lyrics from a nineteenth-century German poem "Mein Vater war ein Wandersmann." Friedrich-Wilhelm Möller, a contemporary German composer, added the music, as Germany too desperately needed sunshine. Möller's sister—in the way that life regularly imitates the movies—ran a children's choir in Northern Germany that included a number of war orphans, and their prize-winning version of the song ultimately reached the BBC, which aired it in 1953. Recorded by British orchestra leader Frank Weir with lyrics translated into English by a Dutch-born writer, "The Happy Wanderer" might help date the dim origins of postmodernism: the song successfully eliminates the defining modernist contrast between surface and depth. "The Happy Wanderer" is all surface.

The version by Frank Weir included his own catchy soprano saxophone solos between verses. If—a big if—"The Happy Wanderer" inspired seven-year-old Bill Clinton in Arkansas to take up the tenor sax, it would have changed American politics, as Clinton's late-night TV performance (in hipster dark glasses) contributed a "cool factor" that rescued his lagging campaign. Someone should ask him.

What I needed in 1954 as a 12-year-old was not a wander in the mountains—the highest point in my home state of Delaware is 450 feet above sea level—but a ride that would spare me the shame of arriving at school on the long yellow bus. "The Happy Wanderer," with its inane but addictive chorus, offered a distraction from the exhausting 50s preteen quest for coolness:

> Val-deri, Val-dera,
> Val-deri,
> Val-dera-ha-ha-ha-ha-ha
> Val-deri, Val-dera.
> My knapsack on my back.[1]

Maybe *val-deri, val-dera* sounds as goofy in French and German as in English—one secret of its international appeal—although the trailing *ha-ha-ha-ha-ha* struck me as demented, which may explain why, stateside, "The Happy Wanderer" sparked a craze for Tyrolean hats. The sloped crown, braided hatbands, and colorful spray of feathers spoke of European mysteries. I did not have whatever it takes to resist: I caved in to the lure of fine feathered alpine headwear. The '60s could not come fast enough.

Nietzsche, a genuine wanderer, liked to take long walks in the mountains. The bracing air matched his startling pronouncements in their cold, posthuman rigor —"God is dead"—that even the Beat Generation existentialists in 1954 didn't quite grasp. His walks, in addition to clearing the mind for philosophy, belonged to his search for relief from multiple maladies. Health (a subject closely linked with his philosophic views) required, if not wandering, at least abandoning the scholar's desk and chair. "*Sit* as little as possible," he advises; "do not believe any idea that was not conceived while moving around outside."[2] The concept he called the "fundamental idea of my work" (probably the Eternal Recurrence) came to him, he recalled later, beside a Swiss mountain lake while he was "wandering through the woods."[3] Wandering—not just walking, as for the ancient Peripatetic school—thus holds a significant place in contemporary philosophy.

Wandering offered Nietzsche not only a stimulus for health and thought but also, most important, an alter ego. His creative breakthrough when wandering by a Swiss lake at 6,000 feet comes as more than an anecdotal curiosity or an unrelated moment of insight, like Archimedes stepping into his bath and ("Eureka!") discovering the law of buoyancy. Zarathustra, Nietzsche's philosophical hero and alter ego, begins a solitary midnight climb by crossing a mountain ridge toward the distant harbor far below, in what constitutes almost a model of Nietzschean thought. "Ich bin ein Wanderer," he muses, "und ein Bergsteiger" (a wanderer and a mountain climber).[4]

Wandering in the dark while climbing at breathtaking altitudes, minus all safety precautions, is not just risky; it constitutes, for Nietzsche, a metaphoric identity: who he is as a philosopher.

Mountain climbers, a breed apart even in daylight, require the skills, stamina, and daredevil or risk-taking mental powers worth remembering when we think of Nietzsche or Zarathustra. They are high-wire wanderers. Mountaineers today climb with the help of specialized gear from boots and crampons to rope, harness, and ice axe: no *Val-deri, Val-dera* excursions. Nietzsche and his alter ego Zarathustra undertake an arduous thinking minus the safety net of absolutes. The oxygen is thin at 6,000 feet; the mean Fahrenheit temperature is five degrees above freezing; crevices and rock slides pose constant danger.

Nietzsche's high-altitude philosophical writing gets expressed in enigmatic, figurative prose that continually challenges readers to hang on. Sense, as readers know it on the lowlands, keeps slipping away. "The Happy Wanderer," almost the musical opposite of philosophy, offers a tuneful postwar wish-fulfillment fantasy: a cheerful outdoors holiday from thought. It is doubtless what conflict-weary transatlantic cultures in the mid-1950s deeply desired. The high-register soprano sax solos even suspend the implicit everyday obligation to enter into language: *Val-deri, val-dera. Val-dera-ha-ha-ha-ha-ha.*

Nietzsche's wanderer makes a meaningful contrast with the 1950s Happy Wanderer, whose signature refrain comes very close to absolute nonsense. Nietzsche, in a far different register, invites readers to challenge ordinary modes of thought and expression that produce what we call sense. His enigmatic and opaque assertions at times press the limits of rational thought. In effect, he invites readers to abandon the Happy Wanderer as an escapist artifact and to imagine—in its most rigorous, joyous archetype as a high-stakes thinker with no safety net and no absolutes—the Philosopher as Wanderer.

Notes

1 "The Happy Wanderer," https://www.scoutsongs.com/lyrics/happywanderer.html.

2 Friedrich Nietzsche, Ecce Homo (1908), in The Anti-Christ, Ecce Homo, Twilight of the Idols and Other Writings, ed. Aaron Ridley and Judith Norman, trans. Judith Norman (Cambridge: Cambridge University Press, 2005), 87. The text was written in 1888.

3 Quoted in Mrs. Förster-Nietzsche, "Introduction," in Thus Spake Zarathustra, trans. Thomas Common (1909), https://www.gutenberg.org/files/1998/1998-h/1998-h.htm#link2H_INTR.

4 Friedrich Nietzsche, Thus Spoke Zarathustra, ed. Adrian Del Caro and Robert Pippin, trans. Adrian Del Caro (Cambridge: Cambridge University Press, 2006), 121. The section entitled "The Wanderer," which begins Part Three and from which this passage derives, appeared in 1884. Part One appeared in 1883; Part Four was added in 1892.

4 Wandering as punishment

God thunders out his curse: "A fugitive and a wanderer shalt thou be in the earth."[1]

Cain, the firstborn son of Adam and Eve, has killed his brother. Now, the first murderer and the first fratricide, he stands on the receiving end of a divine curse. Cain alone with God. Face-to-face. Unmediated. No whirlwind, no burning bush. He has already made the mistake of replying to God's question about Abel's whereabouts with an all-time transparent equivocation: "Am I my brother's keeper?" (4:9). A very big mistake. God asks all the questions, as Job learns too. God, in place of a reply, utters the awful sentence that Cain no doubt hears thereafter even in his sleep: "A fugitive and a wanderer shalt thou be in the earth."

Cain is a biblical archetype of the wanderer. Equally important, it is through Cain that wandering establishes an ancient pedigree as punishment. *Wanderer*, in his case, is less a description than a quasi-legal sentence, and wandering for Cain means exile: a sentence more severe than even the expulsion of Adam and Eve. As the penalty for man's first disobedience, they are expelled from the garden, but not from Eden. They may settle where they please. Cain, a murderer with blood on his hands, is not permitted to settle. He is condemned to wander as an outlaw, an exile, always in motion, without a home or a place to rest (Figure 4.1). He seems to understand instinctively the fate that lies ahead.

"My punishment," he cries out, "is greater than I can bear" (4:13).

The biblical origin of wandering as punishment offers much to ponder. Cain fears that he will be recognized as an exile and killed, and his fear perfectly anticipates the later history of wanderers as vulnerable strangers. Not so, God replies, adding that anyone who harms Cain will suffer vengeance "sevenfold." The math remains unclear, if ominous, but Dante and Hieronymus Bosch could surely sketch in some

DOI: 10.4324/9781003255307-4

Figure 4.1 Henri Vidal. *Cain After Having Killed His Brother Abel* (1896). Jardin des Tuileries, Paris. Archive Timothy McCarthy/Art Resource, NY.

vivid details of divine wrath. The point remains that God intends Cain to survive—and so provides a distinguishing sign that means *hands off.* "And the LORD set a mark on Cain," the biblical narrative adds, "lest any finding him should kill him" (4:15).

The notorious mark of Cain, left unspecified, quickly becomes central to his legend. The Hebrew term translated as "mark" could refer to an invisible omen or to a visible stain or scar. The clear purpose is to identify Cain as both cursed and untouchable: a marked wanderer who must not be killed so that his punishment cannot end. The notorious "mark" meanwhile authorizes a tradition that portrays Cain as a damned and blasted figure, akin to damaged Gothic villains, doomed to wander the earth in perpetual anguish.

Cain, as the ancestor of cursed, desolate, and driven fictive wanderers from the Ancient Mariner to the Flying Dutchman, found some solace among the same Romantic and post-romantic readers who sympathized with Milton's Satan. Byron even writes a closet drama entitled *Cain* (1821), in which Lucifer speaks to Cain (prior to the murder of Abel) and explains the coming history of death that Cain will unleash. The famed Byronic antiheroes almost always carry a Cain-like mark or internal stigma that sets them apart.

Wandering as personified in Cain is more than a punishment. The punishment, in a curious twist, becomes a crime. The King James Version translates the key term in God's curse not as *wanderer* but *vagabond.* Vagabond (from the Latin *vagari*, meaning "to wander") is a tendentious choice in 1611 because vagabonds are, by law, criminals. In 1494, Parliament passes a Vagabonds and Beggars Act, which decrees that vagabonds stand for three days and nights in the stocks, after which they are run out of town.

Wanderers are not criminals, legally speaking, but vagabonds are. They arrive from elsewhere and, especially if run out of town, leave headed elsewhere. A subsequent Vagabonds Act of 1530 specifies that vagabonds be tied to carts and whipped "until the blood streams from their bodies." For a second arrest, authorities repeat the whipping and slice off half an ear. For a third arrest, the offending vagabond proceeds straight to execution. Among the new and slightly more compassionate Elizabethan Poor Laws, Parliament in 1597 provides that convicted vagabonds be deported overseas, just when (coincidentally) English colonies need unpaid laborers.

Vagrant, another legal term that shares the same Latin root as *vagabond*, refers in the Middle Ages to any homeless and unemployed person. The medieval world in Christian countries discriminates between working poor (who merit help) and undeserving vagrants (mostly males who choose not to work). Such laws tend to increase in frequency and harshness during periods of crisis, and one such law in England and Wales—the Ordinance of Labourers (1349)—has the design of increasing the workforce depleted during the Black Death. Idleness is not quite a deadly sin, like sloth, but at times it poses a direct threat to public order. So-called masterless men inspire laws both in England and in America designed at specific periods to prevent the movement of unemployed, homeless men.[2] Vagrancy laws are mostly unconstitutional now, but they survive in some non-Western nations where draconian statutes seek to oppress or eliminate gypsies.

Cain and his fellow vagrants face additional punishments. God curses Cain not only as a wanderer but also as a fugitive. Questions of guilt matter less in the experience of fugitives than a psychology of flight. Fugitives live furtive, anxiety-ridden lives, dodging and weaving, lying low, in disguise or blending into the crowd. As (literally) a marked man, Cain will never blend in, and we might imagine him forever glancing over his shoulder, fearing recognition or capture, his body slumped, as if in abject self-erasure. As a lineal descendant of Cain, the fugitive wanders with a difference, under the psychological burden of perpetual flight, but fugitive wandering also absorbs the divine curse of endlessness. A fugitive, once captured, is no longer a fugitive, so one's status as a fugitive logically entails forever avoiding capture. God is never done punishing Cain—fugitive and wanderer—biblical archetype of the Wanderer as Outlaw.

The curse of endless wandering, for Cain, holds a temporal twist. He not only cannot be killed but also, as biblical tradition has it, cannot die. God sentences Cain to wander the earth, *forever.*

Cain, as a mythic figure of the doomed eternal wanderer, gives rise to multiple avatars who resemble—to alter Joseph Campbell's famous description—an antihero with a thousand faces. The hero's journey, for Campbell, is circular: the hero leaves home on an adventure, overcomes a crisis, and returns home changed.[3] The wanderer's journey, with Cain as the prototype, is linear, open-ended, and static: he wanders out of Eden, overcomes nothing, lives in perpetual torment, endlessly, and never returns. Myths embody contradictions that are social as well as psychological, and wandering construed as both crime and punishment in some sense absolves societies of care for the nameless, often stateless people who wander away from burned-out villages, flooded farmland, and violent, gang-controlled streets and who we call refugees, migrants, or illegal (undocumented) aliens.

Cain also might prompt us to rethink the larger meanings of fratricide. The brotherhood of man—*fraternité*—is a lofty metaphor. We are all, in some ideal sense, our brothers' keepers. Civil society may depend less on social contracts—an obsolete metaphor—than on the care we extend to our metaphoric brothers and sisters. The act of brother-killing-brother is replayed endlessly in civil strife, as Israeli scholar Avner Falk suggests in Fratricide in the Holy Land (2004), and fratricidal conflicts regularly divide families, clans, and even nations.[4] Cain raises questions about how we treat contemporary wanderers who step across the arbitrary, shifting national borders that did not exist when *Homo erectus* first wandered, freely, out of what was not yet called Africa.

Wandering is not always a punishment, despite the power of Cain's example. It can serve at times as a refuge from state power, soft or hard, and offers a pragmatic cloak of invisibility for people who need to slip beneath the radar. A wanderer who possesses no rights of citizenship and no national identity, however, is also always vulnerable to the attacks that Cain rightly feared. Wandering is rarely scot-free. Its virtues and its pleasures entail risk, and even philosophers must descend from the mountaintop. I like to imagine the Happy Wanderer on his hike, singing *val-deri, val-dera* as he begins his descent, then pausing abruptly to peer at a bent figure trudging up the same mountain path. Who could it be? Wanderers are shape-shifters. Cain or his innocent kin might turn up anywhere—wandering—on the endless passage elsewhere. It shouldn't be so hard to extend a hand.

Notes

1 Genesis 4:12. All quotations are from the King James Version (1611) and further quotations are documented within the text. In this case I have substituted *wanderer*, found in many translations of this verse, for the King James translators' choice, discussed later.

2 See A. L. Beier, Masterless Men: The Vagrancy Problem in England 1560–1640 (New York: Methuen, 1985); and Keri Leigh Merritt, Masterless Men: Poor Whites and Slavery in the Antebellulm South (Cambridge: Cambridge University Press, 2017).

3 Joseph Campbell, The Hero With a Thousand Faces (1949), 3rd edn (Novato, CA: New World Library, 2008). Campbell's schema actually distinguishes 17 specific steps or features of the hero's journey.

4 Avner Falk, Fratricide in the Holy Land: A Psychoanalytic View of the Arab-Israeli Conflict (Madison: University of Wisconsin Press, 2004).

5 Nomadlands

"There have always been itinerants, drifters, hobos, restless souls," writes Jessica Bruder in Nomadland (2017), the nonfiction book adapted for the prize-winning 2020 film directed by Chloé Zhao. "But now, in the third millennium, a new kind of wandering tribe is emerging."[1]

These "new nomads," as Bruder calls them, are predominantly elderly, white, retired, often in dire financial straits, and living out of their cars, vans, or camping vehicles. They crisscross the country on the lookout for safe, free overnight parking. In between low-paying, temporary jobs that target mobile workers, some 40,000 van-dwellers—whom Bruder calls "downwardly mobile older Americans" (62)—pack close together on a stretch of arid, deserted public land near the Arizona town of Quartzsite, waiting out the winter. They understand their condition as refugees from the once-potent American dream of home ownership, which has rapidly turned into nightmares of underwater mortgages, foreclosure, and eviction. Some elderly van-dwellers simply prefer wandering adventures on the road to predictable, medical end-of-life decline.

Wanderers are defined by mobility, but the mobility of traditional wanderers plays out mainly in a horizontal, lateral dimension as they move across the countryside. The new van-dwelling nomads, while traversing the flatlands, also occupy a vertical trajectory: straight down, with more falling ahead. Despite a precarious, temporary equilibrium, they remain surprisingly upbeat as they survive on incomes reduced sometimes to a monthly Social Security check—$524 for Linda May, the van-dweller whose life story Bruder recounts. A cracked engine block or worn-out tires can signal disaster, but a national myth of rugged individualism helps them shrug off catastrophe. They mostly adopt the cornered gunslinger's boast that they won't go down without a fight. Nomadland resembles a postindustrial parable played out in

DOI: 10.4324/9781003255307-5

real time, as ageing wanderers pose for photos against actual, if faded, Wild West movie sets, pretending.

Nomadland turns Bruder, as investigative journalist, into a surrogate wanderer, spending months away from her Brooklyn apartment and living in a camper among itinerant elders. She joins them at temporary jobs, conventions, and campgrounds, as they pause (for work or friendship) before hitting the road again. The pauses are less interruptions than momentary rest stops within the staccato rhythm of a van-dwelling life. Bruder drives some 15,000 miles over three years, as she tracks the wandering retirees and housing expats on journeys with no final destination, except death. Single women, hardest hit by recent economic maladies, make up a significant percentage of van-dwellers, and they are out there driving still. They reflect the American romance of the automobile turned inside out and sour, although with a few random redeeming moments, less sweet than bittersweet.

Van-dwellers don't like the term *homeless*, but prefer the euphemism *houseless*. They are right, technically, since most have left brick-and-mortar houses behind and now make their homes in a van. Like home, freedom is a concept they continually invoke but redefine, since (again technically) they are free from mortgages, lawn mowers, and utility bills. The rising price of gasoline, on the other hand, severely limits their freedom. The new gig economy poses another severe limitation. *Workampers*, as they are called, take whatever odd jobs they can find: as ticket-takers at amusement parks, outhouse cleaners at national parks, or shift workers outdoors in the bitter cold, 12 hours running, at an annual sugar beet harvest. It is the limited freedom of marginal, mobile, invisible people, not exactly oppressed but certainly exploited, who take what they can get with no safety net. Sometimes the pay is only free parking, with hookups for water.

Wandering for the average workamper depends upon a vehicle, usually second-hand and in decline, no matter how lovingly tricked out. A few luxury motorhomes join the ranks, but most vehicles serve as cramped escape pods for elderly individuals ejected from a booming economy that has failed them. Alcoholism and drug abuse set some wanderers on their tailspin course after a tragedy like divorce or the death of a spouse. Their vehicles allow them to live off the land, although reduced to dependence on the kindness of strangers when repairs come due. Passing the hat to help a cash-strapped, stranded fellow van-dweller is a prized tradition, but the vehicles pose an ongoing threat beyond breakdown.

The knock. Bruder, writing later in the *New York Times*, isolates the knock as the most terrifying everyday anxiety facing van-dwellers. She experienced such terror firsthand while sleeping overnight parked on city streets. Three sharp raps usually means the police. The knock, Bruder writes, is a visceral, inescapable, existential threat. "How do you avoid it?" she asks. The answer: "You hide in plain sight. Make yourself invisible. Internalize the idea that you're unwelcome. Stay hypervigilant to avoid trouble."[2]

There is a worst-case outcome short of murder. If it is the police who knock, your vehicle gets towed away and impounded. Failure to pay an impound fee means losing your home. Now you are more than houseless. Municipalities meanwhile devise regulations designed specifically to restrict van-dwellers, thus skirting statutes against vagrancy recently declared unconstitutional. The knock, as a fear-generating technique, conveys a larger (if unstated) social desire to outlaw wandering and to treat wanderers with the rough justice that outlaws—mostly elderly, houseless van-dwellers—are said to deserve.

Wandering, as reflected in the van-dweller's way of life, requires a commitment to improvisation. It adopts the indigenous practice of *bricolage*, cobbling together what's needed from whatever lies ready-at-hand. Bedouins set loose their camels and head for a nearby town whenever the desert climate turns too hostile. Van-dwellers in need of cash head for the nearest Amazon fulfillment center.

Amazon, I was surprised to learn, is the largest US employer of nomadic van-dwellers. The digital giant, now the world's fifth-largest employer in the new global economy, scoops up discarded elderly workers and hires them as temporary help. Indeed, since 2008, Amazon has developed an annual, seasonal program called CamperForce that specializes in short-term jobs for older workers living in vans, whom the tech giant prefers for their work ethic and portable housing. Younger applicants now compete for the same jobs, but the old-school workers need the money, accept low wages, don't ask for benefits, avoid union organizers, and leave quietly when the job ends. It can cost around $175 to gas up your van, and seasonal money is manna for the cash-strapped.

Gig work at Amazon has one main downside: it is brutal. As journalistic research, Bruder signs up for a CamperForce job, but quits almost immediately. Linda May suffers a serious repetitive-motion injury from Amazon's heavy hand-scanner—serious enough that she decides never to work there again. Wandering cross-country in a van may feel like freedom, for a while. How free are you, however, spending 12-hour shifts walking 15 miles daily on concrete floors in a warehouse spanning four football fields? The company sets deadlines for the maximum elapsed time allowed as you race to fetch the latest shiny object or get fired. The freedom of the unfree remains a paradox at the heart of the new van-dwelling life.

Linda May, at the beginning of Nomadland, drives a salvaged Jeep Grand Cherokee Laredo—a full-size SUV built on a truck chassis—towing a used fiberglass mini trailer that she nicknames the Squeeze Inn. It measures 13 feet long bumper to hitch, and the 10′ × 6′ living space allows an inch or two of standing headroom. Her toilet is a five-gallon bucket.

Wandering, in the nomadlands stretching beyond the subculture of van-dwellers, has economic, social, and political dimensions that are harder to see than a stealth camper parked in the desert. Alex Domash traveled with a caravan of migrants crossing Mexico toward the US border and sees both South and North Americans as affected by climate change. "Americans," he writes, "are becoming climate migrants before our eyes."[3]

Climate migrants are certainly not adventurers, but, like the van-dwellers, they are not exactly victims either. The new wanderers are taking action within a global economy gripped by rapid change, including climate change. Climates and economies are not the only forces of instability ahead. The earth's magnetic poles flipped 42,000 years ago, with catastrophic changes, possibly wiping out the sedentary Neanderthals. The poles may flip again soon, knocking out electrical grids and satellite networks, so we may all need to relearn the survival skills associated with wandering.[4] The image of globalized nomadlands, however, mostly conjures up a frightening dystopian future that moviegoers will recognize: a *Mad Max* wasteland of armed and desperate wanderers.

Here is a likelier scenario for future wanderers. Your rent is due. Your job has vanished. You're edging toward retirement age. No one wants to hire you. Living in a van may be your best option. You spend your last savings on a battered camper and disappear off the grid, with no insurance and no cash to pay the dentist, so you let your teeth go bad, depend on handouts when your camper breaks down, which it will, dodge the police to find free overnight parking, and shit into a bucket. Bruder meets van-dwelling wanderers who adamantly refuse to return to the failed world of what they call bricks-and-sticks housing. "And that means," she says, "many will have to live in hiding, on and off, until they die" (206).

Notes

1 Jessica Bruder, Nomadland: Surviving America in the Twenty-First Century (New York: Norton, 2017), xii. Further quotations are documented within the text.

2 Jessica Bruder, "I Lived in a Van to Write the Book Behind 'Nomadland.' The Fear Is Real," *New York Times*, 24 April 2021, https://www.nytimes.com/2021/04/24/opinion/nomadland-oscars.html.

3 Alex Domash, “Americans Are Becoming Climate Migrants Before Our Eyes,” *The Guardian*, 2 October 2020, https://www.theguardian.com/commentisfree/2020/oct/02/climate-change-migration-us-wildfires.

4 Nicola Davis, “End of Neanderthals Linked to Flip of Earth’s Magnetic Poles, Study Suggests,” *The Guardian*, 18 February 2021, https://www.theguardian.com/science/2021/feb/18/end-of-neanderthals-linked-to-flip-of-earths-magnetic-poles-study-suggests; and Karina Shah, “Earth’s Magnetic Field Flipping Linked to Extinctions 42,000 Years Ago,” *New Scientist*, 18 February 2021, https://www.newscientist.com/article/2268520-earths-magnetic-field-flipping-linked-to-extinctions-42000-years-ago/.

6 What is called wandering?

Martin Heidegger in 1954 published a slim collection of 21 lectures under the curious title Was Heißt Denken? or, in literal translation, What Is Called Thinking? Hannah Arendt calls it, in a dust jacket blurb, "as important as Being and Time" and "perhaps the most exciting of his books."[1] Heidegger, in a carefully unexciting choice of words, does not ask what thinking *is*. Only what we *call* thinking. He does not seek to uncover an essence of thought: its hidden or forgotten truth. His approach rather is rooted in immediate experience. "We shall never learn what 'is called' swimming, for example, or what it 'calls for,' by reading a treatise on swimming," he writes. "Only the leap into the river tells us what is called swimming."[2]

A leap into wandering cannot explain what wandering *is*, since it too does not lend itself to a search for essences. There is practical value, however, in leaping in to examine singular instances that ask us or call for us to understand wandering one by one. Heidegger, in fact, devotes almost half of What Is Called Thinking? to unfolding a single statement by Parmenides: "It is necessary to say and think that Being is." Wandering, while it might repay a similarly deep plunge into a single episode, also rewards a more extended unfolding that reflects upon its widest distribution across times and cultures.

We understand intuitively how walking differs from crawling, skipping, running, leaping about, and standing still, but what on earth *is* wandering? Suddenly intuition falters and the fog rolls in. Wandering takes us into apparently common but unfamiliar territory, where its ordinariness makes contact with something slightly uncanny—unlike walking, nearly an autonomic function that we learn as infants. "I have met with but one or two persons in the course of my life who understood the art of Walking," Thoreau writes.[3] His deliberately excessive or paradoxical claim, however, simply prepares readers to understand his true, canny (transcendental) Art of Walking.

DOI: 10.4324/9781003255307-6

Wandering in its uncanniness seems always to withhold full understanding. Freud, in his reflections on the uncanny, might suggest that wandering in its casual everydayness—deeply familiar but also strangely unknown—makes contact with unconscious, forgotten, or repressed desires. Wandering holds a power to exert (at unpredictable times and places) a mysterious *call.*

Carl Sagan is surely right: humans once were wanderers and perhaps, even at some buried level of being, we still are. Wandering, like the uncanny, can also evoke vaguely sinister or unsettling responses, although again we don't quite know why. Ancient peoples certainly understood that wandering, like other forced or unforced relocations, does not always promise a good outcome.

"Wandering among people with dementia," advises the Alzheimer's Association, "is dangerous…."[4] Dementia patients in assisted living facilities, as a recent study shows, move around in "wandering patterns" and "wandering trajectories" that are random and illogical.[5] Some years ago, I arrived home to find a police car in the driveway. The officers had stopped my wife—not yet diagnosed with younger onset Alzheimer's disease—as she was driving north in the southbound lane of a busy divided highway.

Wayfinding, the opposite of getting lost or disoriented, is a basic psychological function that everyone relies on. The human brain in its normal state, as neurologists might say, wants to find its way home. Navigational grid cells in the brain—a likely aid in wayfinding—are often damaged in the early stages of Alzheimer's disease.[6] Our survival as a species no doubt once depended on wayfinding. Compasses, maps, and smart phones now substitute for grid cells, but few people can wander hopelessly lost for long periods without terror. In an age-old wisdom of the body, a good many people seem to avoid wandering altogether. It is important not to romanticize a desire to wander, no matter its attraction for Romantic poets, but to stay alert to its dangers and discontents.

In the long game of evolution, wandering no doubt confers value in advancing human survival, maybe even adaptive value. Most people also need an occasional vacation from logic, routine, and the obligations to earn a livelihood. Who doesn't enjoy letting go and entering, briefly, into a period of carnival excess? Carnivals can turn dangerous, however, like wandering. We do not normally linger long in wandering trajectories if we can help it, but sometimes we can't help it and sometimes we just need to hit the road.

"I travel not to go anywhere, but to go. I travel for travel's sake," writes the novelist Robert Louis Stevenson. "The great affair is to move...."[7] Stevenson, then in his 20s, needed to break free from a doomed love affair, but he also reflects a widely shared desire. The meaty German noun *Wanderlust* signifies a drive to keep moving on, much like travel for travel's sake. *Fernweh* in German refers to an ache or pain for a distant place where you feel you belong.[8] A longing to be where you belong, even in a local bar where everybody knows your name, is the flip side of a terror at getting lost—with no way home, with nowhere to belong.

The widely shared desire for a settled homeland constitutes the psychic opposite of wanderlust. *Husband* and *husbandry* derive from an Old English compound that means "house-dweller." It is farmers who dwelled in houses, tended crops, and heralded the future, while knights, hermits, mendicants, and shepherds wandered.

Whatever wandering is or is called, which remains undetermined, might begin with this observation. Wandering is a patternless action unfolding over time that differs from the common purposes of walking. Not all who wander are lost, as readers recall from Lord of the Rings, and not all who wander are called *wanderers*.[9] Alzheimer's patients wander, but they are not called wanderers. Lost children wander, but they are not called wanderers. The social and linguistic category *wanderer* requires more than the action of wandering. Doctors, teachers, and students all write, but they are not called writers. It is still unclear what social magic occurs to transform a person who wanders into a wanderer, but it likely involves duration and patternlessness.

A leap into the historical flow of wandering—necessary to follow the irregular, twisting pathways of actual or fictive wanderers—is beset with difficulties. A suburbanite strolling with a pet dog wanders in a register different from that of a fictional character (created by a major twentieth-century philosopher) climbing a mountain at midnight. A leap into the stream suggests that wandering will not reveal its truths to an inquiry based on the application of logic and reason alone. There is no essence to uncover.

Whatever we call wandering, it remains a primordial, recurrent, and uncanny human experience, capable of evoking the stone-cold terror of getting lost or the heartwarming expectation of finding your way home. The narratives, discourses, and cultural artifacts that help us understand it do not belong to literature or language alone but include material roads and pathless woods. Just as material roads include potholes and dead ends, however, so too *the road* as a traditional figure of speech or textual feature proves porous, indeterminate, and subject to semantic blockages.[10] Robert Frost's road "less traveled by" may not refer to a material road at all, or else evokes a road as the verbal sign of experiences too complex for language. Bob Dylan's question of how many roads a man must walk down is not primarily about asphalt or gait, although it may evoke in listeners their individual memories of material roads and actual walks, or possibly the social dilemma of whatever it takes to be "called" a man. It does not fatally disable or subvert understanding if meanings expand to fill the available space of interpretation. The terms *wanderers* and *wandering* are intrinsically rich and opaque, especially as they shift into metaphor, and surplus difficulties are precisely what to expect when we leap headlong into the stream.

Wandering is what humans do, much as we dither or drift or find our way home in the dark. It lies behind the dreams of one day finding the forgotten place where we truly belong and also behind the nightmare that one day we may wake up homeless, jobless, rootless, with nowhere to turn except to the road, as many elderly van-dwellers do, living in a 10′ × 6′ camper, feeling perhaps like an adult child lost in the woods.

Notes

1 Quoted on the back cover of Martin Heidegger, What Is Called Thinking? (1954), trans. Fred D. Wieck and J. Glenn Gray (New York: Harper & Row, 1968).
2 Heidegger, What Is Called Thinking?, trans. Wieck and Gray, 21.
3 Henry David Thoreau, "Walking" (1862), in Excursions, ed. Joseph J. Moldenhauer (Princeton: Princeton University Press, 2007), 243.
4 "Stages & Behaviors," Alzheimer's Association, https://www.alz.org/help-support/caregiving/stages-behaviors.
5 Edgar Batista, Frederic Borras, Fran Casino, and Agusti Solanas, "A Study on the Detection of Wandering Patterns in Human Trajectories," 6th International Conference on Information, Intelligence, Systems and Applications (IISA), 2015, https://ieeexplore.ieee.org/document/7387995.
6 James Gorman, "Navigational Cells Located in Human Brains," *New York Times*, 4 August 2013, https://www.nytimes.com/2013/08/06/science/navigational-cell-systems-located-in-human-brains.html.
7 Robert Louis Stevenson, Travels with a Donkey in the Cévennes (1879; rpt. New York: The Heritage Press, 1957), 51.
8 Xiaolu Guo, A Lover's Discourse (New York: Grove Press, 2020), 138–139.
9 J.R.R. Tolkien, The Fellowship of the Ring (1954; rpt. New York: Houghton Mifflin Harcourt, 1994), 241.
10 See, for a lucid account of the difficulties, Christopher D. Morris, The Figure of the Road: Deconstructive Studies in Humanities Disciplines (New York: Peter Lang, 2007).

7 I'm going nowhere

Dwight D. Eisenhower, five-star general and former supreme commander of NATO, assumes the US presidency in January 1953, shortly before Nikita Khrushchev takes power in the USSR as first secretary of the Communist Party. An armed standoff between two hostile nuclear powers might well inspire fantasies of wandering off. In 1954, as if hearing the call to move on, 19-year-old Elvis Presley releases his first record, "That's All Right." With his transgressive hips and delinquent good looks, he is "covering"—for young white audiences—a song written and recorded a decade earlier by a middle-aged black singer-songwriter, Arthur Crudup. Step aside, Crudup. Roll over, Beethoven. Music, race, media, and mass culture have wandered into a turning point.

What's in a name? Television is the new media of the 1950s, and in 1956 a youthful radio disc jockey and television personality named Dick Clark—Richard Augustus Wagstaff Clark, Jr.—takes over a local after-school dance program and propels it to national stardom as *American Bandstand.* It is a machine for manufacturing teen idols. Walden Cassotto, Francis Avallone, and Robert Ridarelli soon headline the rotating cast of white heartthrobs who service the teenage music market, mixed with occasional black doo-wop groups. Cassotto, Avallone, and Ridarelli all adopt ethnically-neutral, airbrushed names—Bobby Darin, Frankie Avalon, and Bobby Rydell—as does the South Philly dreamboat Fabiano Forte, who records simply as Fabian. Prominent among the manufactured teen icons is a genuinely talented young musician, Dion DiMucci (Figure 7.1), who contracts his given name to the single brand-like, resonant, and innocuous melting-pot disyllable Dion.

Winsome smile, dark pompadour, and deep brown eyes give Dion the perfect swoon-worthy look to accompany the pop-rock song he releases in 1961, "The Wanderer."

DOI: 10.4324/9781003255307-7

Figure 7.1 *Dion: Lovers Who Wander* (1962). Detail. Album Cover. Courtesy of ABM Records. Photo: David Morris.

The Wanderer as Lover, who doubles as the archetypal Lover as Wanderer, embraces a variety of mostly male serial paramours, in contrast to courtly or domestic traditions of faithful lovers who do not wander. Some erotic wanderers are little more than charming rogues or aristocratic predators. Classic seducers such as Giacomo Casanova and Don Juan moved through women like roving sex addicts or, at least, like seducers addicted to the art of seduction. Dion's "The Wanderer" offers a less pathological version of the roving serial lover, which nonetheless runs counter to the prevailing bourgeois morality of love and marriage, already beginning to look somewhat tattered as the divorce rates climb. Frank Sinatra, in a televised remake of Thornton Wilder's play *Our Town*, sings a saccharine ballad celebrating monogamy titled "Love and Marriage." He releases it as a hit single in 1955, on his way to four marriages and numerous extramarital affairs.

Dion, with his wholesome smile and cuddly sweater, does not edge far into the danger zone marked out by Elvis, nor does his mom-friendly demeanor hint at the gender trouble lying ahead. His teen wanderer, however, while at a safe distance from the approaching sex-and-drugs music scene, expresses a view of "pretty girls" that aptly defines the blindfold mentality linking serial seducers past and future: "to me they're all the same."[1]

Wandering, in this musical seduction, is not simply an action but an identity: "They call me the wanderer." Dion's song, despite its follies, not only transforms wandering into a public persona but also identifies male wanderers with a new technology of seduction: the car. Even before it becomes the West Coast icon of male self-display and freedom, the car offers an advantage to wandering lovers that proves almost indispensable. It is not only a gleaming accessory—projecting ultra-desirable qualities—but also a mobile privacy booth, providing a retreat for undisturbed erotic exploits. Drive-in movies are even then forging a new alliance among teen Eros, film, and a subculture of cars. The automobile actually serves multiple purposes for the Wanderer in providing (as for bank robbers) a getaway vehicle: "And when I find myself a-fallin' for some girl, yeah/ I hop right into that car of mine and drive around the world…." The wanderers in Jack Kerouac's On the Road (1957) drive north to south, east to west, and back again in an existential quest as free-flowing as its jazz soundtrack. Dion as Wanderer just zips off to find another chick.

"The Wanderer" doesn't change anything—it's just another catchy 1960s rock anthem. It does, however, reflect a significantly unstable moment of transition. Its erotic ethos seems worrisome enough that record company executives (concerned about sales) insert a last minute revision. DiMucci, years later, calls special attention to the revision, as if it were a saving grace. "But you know," he says, "'The Wanderer' is really a sad song." The sadness, in his revisionist history, emerges in the last-minute change that erases an offending beer bottle. The stanza originally ends touting "my two fists of iron and my bottle of beer." Here is the stanza as the suits revise it:

> Oh well I roam from town to town
> I go through life without a care
> And I'm as happy as a clown
> With my two fists of iron but I'm going nowhere….

Going nowhere? "In the fifties, you didn't get that dark," DiMucci says, reflecting on his signature hit, perhaps briefly forgetting its 1961 release date. "It sounds like a lot of fun, but it's about going nowhere."[2]

Well, maybe. Bruce Springsteen agrees. But the twin guitar sound and double sax beat aren't exactly downcast. Existential sadness seems a stretch. "I'm going nowhere"—as perhaps a flash of introspection—certainly lacks the terse, summary power with which Captain America, a few years later, evaluates the failed existential quest for freedom in the classic 1969 motorcycle-riding buddy film *Easy Rider*: "We blew it."

After 15 years as a self-confessed heroin addict, DiMucci emerges as a born-again Christian, exploring musical styles from blues to gospel, and it is fair to question his reborn assessment of "The Wanderer." *I'm going nowhere*—as the one-off replacement for a beer bottle—perfectly embodies the market-based, sales-happy contradictions of a mainstream music industry that celebrates the bad boy glamour that it pretends to disapprove of: wandering as its own punishment. Wink. Wink. "The Wanderer" in its Portuguese version is entitled "O Lobo Mau," which translates roughly as "The Big Bad Wolf." Badness counts far more than sadness in the identity and appeal of erotic wanderers, which may account for an uncanny sense that we have seen this character before.

"Such is the end of the evildoer: the death of a sinner always reflects his life." So proclaims the libretto as a lightning bolt dispatches Mozart's Don Giovanni to hell.[3] The Italian title of Mozart's opera, *Il dissoluto punito*, reflects a long tradition in which rakes are punished, while "The Wanderer" represents its singing protagonist as neither dissolute nor sinful—only, if you believe Dion, going nowhere. Erotic wandering in 1961 has not yet reached the point when a groupie-fueled, sex-and-drugs lifestyle is simply what rock superstars expect. Dion could claim that he balanced the scales of gender, if slightly, with his companion song about a footloose female wanderer, "Runaround Sue." Fellow males are duly warned to "stay away" from Sue. Females, however, get no such warning to avoid the Wanderer. It is clear which song earns Dion admission into the Rock and Roll Hall of Fame.

"The Wanderer" ranks number 243 on *Rolling Stone* magazine's 2004 list of the *500 Greatest Songs of All Time*. No wanderer and no longer a teen idol but a respected serious musician, Dion DiMucci married Susan Butterfield back in 1963 in a union that has lasted—in defiance of rock norms—well over 50 years.

Notes

1 Dion DiMucci, "The Wanderer," https://genius.com/Dion-the-wanderer-lyrics. "The Wanderer," with lyrics by Ernie Maresca, appears on Dion's album *Runaround Sue* (1961).

2 Quoted in Jack Doyle, "Dion DiMucci, 1950s–2012," *The Pop History Dig*, 11 January 2013, https://www.pophistorydig.com/topics/dion-dimucci-1950s-2012/.

3 Wolfgang Amadeus Mozart, *Don Giovanni* (1787), http://www.murashev.com/opera/Don_Giovanni_libretto_Italian_English.

8 Nomad thought

It's almost midnight ("Um Mitternacht") when Zarathustra, self-described wanderer and mountain climber, ascends in darkness the highest ridge of a mountain he needs to cross in order to reach the distant harbor below. Zarathustra's midnight climb is difficult not to interpret as a Nietzschean metaphor of the modern philosopher's task.

Wandering is not simply physical movement through space. *Nomad thought* is the term philosopher Gilles Deleuze applies to the unsystematic and radical thinking of Friedrich Nietzsche.[1] Nietzsche, creator and sometime alter ego of his philosophical wanderer Zarathustra, undertakes the challenge of rethinking human life unmoored from absolutes. This unmoored, nomadic disposition has a parallel in his own life. After an illness in 1879 that prompts his resignation (at age 34) from his faculty position at the University of Basel, Nietzsche lives in a manner that resembles a restless, nomadic journey and spends his remaining ten years of productive work in "a wandering, gypsy-like existence."[2] He gives up German citizenship, moving between his mother's house in Naumburg and various French, Swiss, German, and Italian cities. As Deleuze describes it, he lives like "a nomad, reduced to a shadow, moving from furnished room to furnished room" (149).

Nietzsche's decade of work and restless wandering, from 1879 to 1889, accounts for almost all the major writing in which he sets orthodox Western thinking on its heels.

What Nietzsche calls his "indescribably strange and dangerous" thinking—strange in its stylistics and dangerous in its assault on traditional values—immerses readers in a foundationless world where truths (as traditionalists call them) are little more than "illusions of which one has forgotten that they are illusions."[3] His radical rethinking calls for a radical style, and Nietzsche favors a philosophical discourse that abandons a logic-driven, argument-heavy analysis for language spiked with metaphors, maxims, parody, ambiguities, fables,

DOI: 10.4324/9781003255307-8

hyperbole, aphorisms, humor, paradox, scorn, and all manner of extravagant language.

Nietzsche's wandering, body-centered, free-form writings cannot be reduced to concepts. What concept can capture the aroma of coffee or the first light of dawn? He has no patience with traditional philosophical reasoning as a means of discovering truth, since in his view such reasoning regularly turns out to support traditional verities. "If someone hides a thing behind a bush, then looks for it and finds it again in the same place," as he mocks traditional reason-based, truth-seeking philosophies, "the seeking and finding are not much to brag about; yet this is how matters stand with the seeking and finding of 'truth' in the realm of reason."[4]

Nomad thought, as Deleuze applies the term to Nietzsche, does not refer to a codified body of beliefs, but rather to a manner of thinking. It is a manner that deliberately seeks to disrupt established codes or doctrines, while taking the even more radical step of embracing the uncodifiable. This process, as Deleuze explains it, offers a fundamental contrast with the work of two other giants of modern thought, Marx and Freud, who dismantle settled codes in political economy and in psychology. Their dismantling operations, however, proceed alongside the creation of what become (at least for their followers) new orthodoxies: Marxism and Freudianism. Nietzsche does not sponsor a new orthodoxy. There is no Nietzscheanism, and followers proceed at their own risk. Nietzsche also takes care to avoid the label *nihilist.* (It describes, after all, another code.) Code-making interests him far less than thinking rooted in extreme states of lived bodily experience, which might be called intensities. Intensities, unlike coded abstractions that merely "represent" experience, demand for Nietzsche a distinctive, disruptive philosophical style. "In his own pulsional form of writing," Deleuze writes, "Nietzsche tells us not to barter away intensity for mere representations" (146).

Wandering has its own peculiar intensities that come with abandoning the standard, approved, straightforward paths. More than a movement outside norms—a stepping aside from orthodoxies and ideologies—it constitutes an outsider position that offers its own alternative strengths. Wandering, in its Nietzschean mode, affirms the value of immediate, un-abstracted, uncodified experience. It extends thinking beyond the calculations of reason to embrace an embodied engagement stripped of traditional preconceptions, absolutes, and social values, open to a wide-ranging revaluation of values and to the encounter with whatever brief or extended intensities lie ahead.

Nietzsche's nomad thought proves revolutionary, in Deleuze's account, because in disrupting settled codes it leads to (or underwrites) the possibility of breakaway movements: departures marked by large numbers of like-minded people actively *opposing* the illusory representations promoted by despotic states and by authoritative structures. "Whole groups depart," as Deleuze describes the exodus: "they become nomads" (148).

Deleuze's own "representation" of Nietzsche as a philosopher of nomad thought—resistant to settled codes—is, of course, questionable as reflecting wider leftist political and quasi-political predilections in contemporary French society. (His essay appears just five years after the notorious student uprising of 1968.) Deleuze may also recruit Nietzsche in support of a desire to free philosophy, at least in its professional versions, from implicit state sponsorship. That is, nomad thinking for Deleuze frees philosophers from complicity with the rationalist ideologies almost synonymous with national governments. "Philosophic discourse," he writes, perhaps referring to ancient Greece, "is born out of the imperial state...."

Nomad philosophers evade both imperial codes and imperial states. Evasion is key. In wandering away from all settled codes in search of a thinking revitalized by intensities, Nietzsche offers an alternative to what Deleuze calls "the utterances of a rational, administrative machinery, whose philosophers would be bureaucrats of pure reason" (149). It is an alternative that holds deep attractions for Deleuze, who in collaboration with psychotherapist Félix Guattari publishes—in A Thousand Plateaus (1980)—a groundbreaking "Treatise on Nomadology."

A sustained anti-rational, anti-imperial politics of wandering, despite a hope for breakaway moments, remains as hard to imagine as a sustained philosophy of wandering. When whole groups depart, new laws and new quasi-Mosaic codes tend to emerge, if only as an alternative to Sadean anarchies or cult-style despotisms. Nietzsche, while an influential figure in the history of philosophy, seems as unlikely as Thoreau to serve as a group leader. (Emerson regretted that Thoreau restricted his ambitions to serving as the captain of huckleberry-gathering parties.) The cold and difficult Nietzschean climb toward an altitude without absolutes leaves many readers unmoved. It is not a realm suitable for dwelling, which is exactly the point. Extended dwelling is not the primary aim of nomads or of nomadic thinking. Even Moses, as he led the Israelites into the desert, faced steady backsliding. The mountain-climbing wanderer Zarathustra (given to bursts of wild Dionysian laughter) proves a disconcerting, unreliable guide to residential living.

Wallace Stevens, like Nietzsche a prodigious walker, submerged his engagement with Nietzschean thought in subtextual relations that are sometimes openly hostile.[5] There is no more significant Nietzschean moment in Stevens's work, however, than when he—in his poetic credo "Of Modern Poetry" (1942)—describes the poet as a "metaphysician in the dark." Nietzsche, of course, has no time for metaphysicians, in darkness or light, but the modern poet for Stevens is similarly deprived of traditional verities and engaged in seeking new paths. Where beauty and truth are no longer shared values or viable poetic standards, Stevens is searching for a poem that marks a significant departure or breakaway, stripped of illusions but open to fictions: "The poem of the mind in the act of finding/ What will suffice."

Stevens's modern poet—a nomadic thinker—adopts a Nietzschean position as metaphoric wanderer: unmoored, removed from traditional certainties, assigning an unsecured (but necessary) value to imagination as replacing an unsustainable religious faith, perhaps capable of no more than limited affirmations or fleeting intensities, which therefore gain special worth. Inhabiting a changed landscape for poetry and thought, where homely jars and ceramic angels replace Keatsian urns, the poet for Stevens seeks whatever the imagination, in its intensities, can transform into an inexplicable, uncodifiable, bare minimum sufficiency, if only "a man skating, a woman dancing, a woman/ Combing."[6]

Notes

1 Gilles Deleuze, "Nomad Thought," in The New Nietzsche, ed. David B. Allison (Cambridge, MA: MIT Press, 1985), 142–149. "*Pensée nomade*," translated here by David B. Allison, first appeared in 1973. Further quotations are documented within the text.

2 "Nietzsche's Life and Works," (1997, revised 2017), in Stanford Encyclopedia of Philosophy, https://plato.stanford.edu/entries/nietzsche-life-works.

3 Nietzsche, "On Truth and Lie in a Nonmoral Sense" (1873), in On Truth and Untruth: Selected Writings, trans. Taylor Carman (New York: HarperCollins, 2010), 30.

4 Nietzsche, "On Truth and Lie in a Nonmoral Sense," in On Truth and Untruth, trans. Carman, 34.

5 B. J. Leggett, Early Stevens: The Nietzschean Intertext (Durham, NC: Duke University Press, 1992). Leggett focuses less on Stevens's specific sources—always debatable—than on "writing in the 'tradition' of Nietzsche" (50).

6 Wallace Stevens, "Of Modern Poetry," in The Collected Poems of Wallace Stevens: The Corrected Edition, ed. John N. Serio and Chris Beyers (New York: Vintage Books, 2015). The original collected edition (uncorrected) was first published in 1954.

9 Sideward glances

We live in an Age of Theory. One gain, offsetting the loss of a common language, is the retreat from assumption-free knowledge. The problem remains that assumptions proliferate, like theorists. My preference among theorists lies with Russian sociolinguist Mikhail Bakhtin, who in the Stalinist era focuses on the hybrid mixtures of dialects and voices that he calls *heteroglossia*.[1] The value of heteroglossia, for Bakhtin, resides in its dialogical power to subvert the authority of monological voices, such as party-line edicts. Its dialogical style not only takes account of other voices—for example, current readers, past writers, and future audiences—but also often employs a "double-voiced" style that embodies multiple perspectives, values, and voices. Speech and writing, for Bakhtin, always incorporate or acknowledge—in extremely complex ways—the often hidden language of the other.

Bakhtin sometimes describes the hidden otherness incorporated or acknowledged in particular acts of speech and writing as reflecting what he calls a "sideward glance."[2] Wandering too incorporates an otherness—Cain, after all, is the first known wanderer—and its overlap with related concepts suggests a sideward glance that acknowledges its kinship with walking, journeys, exile, migration, travel, and similar forms of movement. Wanderers, in effect, recognize that they fall outside the homogeneous patterns that shape settled lives. They inhabit a heterodox or hybrid space that is always mixed. Wandering is an automatic outlier. It stands outside or in resistance to summary statements or settled generalizations seeking to define and confine it, which always absorb a degree of insufficiency that entails its own peculiar sideward glance. Wandering may, in fact, reward a series of sideward glances appropriate to a discontinuous, hybrid activity with all the repose of a wobbling, spinning whirligig.

Glance one. *Wandering, while often played out on the ground, is also performed in the mind.* Walkers often meditate and ruminate,

DOI: 10.4324/9781003255307-9

but walking in its step-by-step performance has long served as a metaphor of logical, sequential thought. Wandering, since it is not restricted to pedestrians, underwrites a different form of mental accompaniment that tends to favor drifting, daydreaming, and sideward glances. Although this general contrast need not hold for individual walkers and wanderers, it remains useful in calling attention to the cognitive activity—emotional as well as rational—that accompanies the otherwise often denigrated act of wandering. What matters most in wandering is the mentality of the wanderer. Wanderers occupy a mental space as distinctive as dreams or daydreams. Lewis and Clark had a job to do, and they did it. As explorers, they explored; they walked but did not "take a walk"; they got lost but did not wander.

Glance two. *Wandering is just what we do when (for an extended period) we move around aimlessly.* Of course, we often move around without a specific purpose. What transforms such purposeless movement into wandering is both its duration and its renegade detachment from the prevailing economic frame of work, production, and added value. It sometimes rides the wave of aimlessness into a counter-economy of pleasure. Walking, of course, can feel pleasant, but a walk is also something you *take*: a goal-driven action, even if the goal is pleasure. Walking, even if brief, usually squeezes in a beginning, middle, and conclusion. It constitutes a mini-narrative. Wandering, in its daydream and drift, offers a break from purpose, which is why wanderers tend to get in trouble. No purpose looks like a bad purpose. Wanderers give the place, as shopkeepers say, a bad name. Wandering is not progress (Latin *pro* + *gradus*, "step"). It is not a step forward, but it is also not falling, not stopping, not pushing. In a Zen-like non-attachment, it can embrace a peaceful, aimless *letting be.*

Glance three. *Wanderers are often invisible.* Am I forgetting the migrants even now, with deadly serious purpose and direction, on the move in a perilous journey across jungles and rivers? Wanderers, while often invisible as individuals, tend to attract notice as a group and threaten the status quo, like homeless vets sleeping on benches near the bus station. The police may have to intervene. ("Move on.") Wanderers thus prefer to slip beneath notice. The wanderer who *just passes through* doesn't stand out or risk becoming a local celebrity. Thoreau, savoring the ironies, writes that he "travelled a good deal" in Concord.[3] He was also well known and well connected, even inventing an improved graphite mix for the family pencil factory. Wanderers who are unemployed, unconnected, and aimless had best move on. They need to be invisible.

Glance four. *Wandering is inimical to the capitalist work ethic and affirms a transgressive counter-ethic.* "He has no time," Thoreau writes of the laborer, "to be any thing but a machine."[4] Today, the travel industry gobbles up much of what remains of our leisure time, converting it into profits. Emerson, who traveled extensively on lecture tours, had no sympathy with leisure travel. "Travelling is a fool's paradise," he writes. "The soul is no traveller: the wise man stays at home…."[5] Wanderers, in what capitalists regard as an act of professional folly or economic suicide, do not command billable hours. They punch no time clock—an invention that dates from 1890 and the origins of modern industrialism. They do not improve the shining hours but prefer to meander, stroll, roam, and pass the time. Some acts of wandering are so inconsequential that, like dreams, they slip from memory, unnoticed. Dreamers, like wanderers, are clock-free and unproductive. No boss wants a worker who wanders the factory floor daydreaming.

Glance five. *Wanderers respect the value of wasting time and other irrational expenditures.* Georges Bataille (1897–1962) described a special kind of waste that he calls *dépense*. *Dépense* for Bataille does not refer to industrial byproducts or discarded materials: the usual detritus of capitalist production. Instead, *dépense* refers to irrational, excessive, extravagant expenditures. It is waste reconfigured as deliberate, outrageous glut, and surfeit, with no redeeming economic advantage. *Dépense*, from lavish ritual gifts in indigenous cultures to primal human blood sacrifice, signifies a profligate expenditure: surplus loss and hyper-waste. It is reckless, senseless consumption, as if a bridegroom set the forest on fire as an over-the-top wedding present. As Bataille explains: "the accent is placed on a *loss* that must be as great as possible in order for that activity to take on its true meaning."[6] Wanderers squander the time, recklessly and irresponsibly. They expect no returns on their disinvestment.

Sideward glances never tell the whole story. They acknowledge part of the story—a part often omitted or even unrecognized—but they do not add up to a summary statement. They are as untheoretical as wandering. Wandering is forever crooked, off message, missing the target, and a colossal waste of time. There is no app to measure it. Wanderers belong to a realm of the immeasurable. They don't need smart watches because time is something they waste, which is not very smart. They do not keep a schedule; they don't have a to-do list; they threw away (or forgot to order) their appointment books. They have no interest in the proposition that time is money or in the project of building up generational wealth. Wanderers, in return for their wasteful litany of refusals and excess, inhabit a sideways mental space that is relatively free, dreamlike, open-ended, and rich with diminished possibilities.

Notes

1 M. M. Bakhtin, The Dialogic Imagination: Four Essays, ed. Michael Holquist, trans. Caryl Emerson and Michael Holquist (Austin: University of Texas Press, 1981). On an age of theory, see François Cusset, French Theory: How Foucault, Derrida, Deleuze, & Co. Transformed the Intellectual Life of the United States (2003), trans. Jeff Fort with Josephine Berganza and Marlon Jones (Minneapolis: University of Minnesota Press, 2008).

2 M. M. Bakhtin, Problems of Dostoevsky's Poetics (1929/1963), ed. and trans. Caryl Emerson (Minneapolis: University of Minnesota Press, 1984), 196. John Cook argues that the Russian phrase should be translated as "backward glance," but it may be hard to overturn current usage, which I follow here ("Glances and Loopholes: Bakhtin's View of Dostoevsky's Linguistic Microcosm," *The Dostoevsky Journal* 19, no. 1 [2018]: 47–71).

3 Henry David Thoreau, Walden (1854), ed. Jeffrey S. Cramer (New Haven, CT: Yale University Press, 2004), 2.

4 Thoreau, Walden, ed. Cramer, 5.

5 Ralph Waldo Emerson, "Self-Reliance" (1841), in Essays by Ralph Waldo Emerson, Introduction by Irwin Edman (1926; rpt. New York: Harper Perennial, 1951), 59. This single volume contains both the First Series (1841) and the Second Series (1844).

6 Georges Bataille, "The Notion of Expenditure" (1933), in The Bataille Reader, ed. Fred Botting and Scott Wilson (Oxford: Blackwell, 1997), 169.

10 Mind-wandering

We spend about 50% of our conscious, waking hours doing whatever it is we do when our minds wander. Mind-wandering, now a technical term in modern cognitive psychology and neuroscience, gets variously defined, but it always refers to whatever it is that happens when we lose mental focus and drift toward a state of daydream or distraction.[1]

The ancient debate about the relation between minds and bodies—entities traditionally regarded as split in a dualism that long predates and follows Descartes—still bedevils current thinking. I believe that minds are always embodied and that bodies are necessary to produce minds, which makes me a monist or at least a non-dualist. Minds, further, are not mysteriously disembodied reasoning machines, running on a calculus of pure logic. Instead, human cognition (as always embodied) is necessarily colored by input from emotion, sensation, memory, habit, and various nonconscious processes. This belief finds increasing support today.

Philosophers and neuroscientists, while still finding areas for disagreement, have recently begun to agree on the concept of an embodied mind.[2] Neural networks communicating in continuous mind/body feedback loops have replaced the old-school fantasy of a tiny person in the brain—the famous *homunculus*—as distinct from the body as the engineer is from the locomotive. Minds and bodies, in short, wander together. The wandering mind is always embodied, limited, and enabled by the brain, drawing upon nonconscious as well as conscious resources. Mind-wandering is thus far more than a metaphor. It describes what the human brain is built to do, and it depends on bodily processes—from neurotransmission to rapid eye movements—even if we don't wander outdoors but recline on a sofa remembering what it was once like to wander.

Whatever humans spend about 50% of their conscious time doing—as we do when mind-wandering—is not an anomaly or glitch or moral

DOI: 10.4324/9781003255307-10

failure. Poets have long taken it seriously, much like Wordsworth remembering a surprise encounter with a host of dancing daffodils:

> For oft, when on my couch I lie
> In vacant or in pensive mood,
> They flash upon that inward eye
> Which is the bliss of solitude....[3]

Wordsworth used the term *recollection* to describe such combined mental-emotional activities, but mind-wandering works too. Minds and bodies, inseparable in their changing relations, may not wander in lockstep, but they always wander together.

The neglected importance of mind-wandering can be summed up in simple arithmetic. We spend on average two hours every night dreaming. These nighttime hours—added to our standard 50%—suggests that we devote nearly two-thirds of our lives to conscious and nonconscious mind-wandering. It's hard to imagine enough time left in the day to put astronauts on the moon. The control room at NASA is, of course, strung tight with directed attention. Perhaps control-room attention is so demanding that the brain needs mind-wandering downtime for recovery. Psychologists are increasingly interested in such nondirected, nonconscious processes, from habits to automatic functions.[4] If daydreaming isn't advisable while hiking the Pacific Crest Trail, where inattention may break a leg, mind-wandering at times may help us survive, as it seemed to do for Jean-Dominique Bauby. His extended near-death experience suggests that mind-wandering may indeed possess survival value.

"I loved to travel," writes Bauby, a 43-year-old magazine editor living the good life outside Paris.[5] One day, while he is taking a German luxury car on a test drive, a sudden massive brainstem injury puts him in a coma. He wakes up some four weeks later just as his left eye is being sewn shut. Once fully conscious, he discovers that he is completely paralyzed. A rare condition called locked-in syndrome leaves him immobile except for a blinking movement in his right eye. "[T]he life I once knew," he later explains, "was snuffed out Friday, the eighth of December, last year" (3).

Bauby, as he adjusts to his near-vegetative state, discovers that he can spell out words, letter-by-letter, blinking in a yes/no code while a speech therapist runs her finger down an alphabetic letter-frequency chart. Somehow he manages to blink out the astonishing brief memoir that consists of what he calls "bedridden travel notes" (5). His travel now occurs only in bed, but his bed is simply the material platform from which his mind still wanders, especially at night. "You can wander off in space or in time," he writes of his nightly mental excursions, "set out for Tierra del Fuego or for King Midas's court" (103). King Midas's court is, of course, a fiction, existing in the imagination, where only brain-based functions prevent it from slipping into nothingness. The brain can take us to places that don't exist. It can parachute us down on a nineteenth-century battlefield or teleport us to Saturn.

Alpha waves increase in the frontal lobes when the mind wanders, according to a team of researchers at UC Berkeley.[6] Do alpha waves decrease if we *walk* to Tierra del Fuego? Bauby's frontal lobes may have hosted massive alpha wave parties as he embarked on his mental travels: "You can visit the woman you love, slide down beside her and stroke her still-sleeping face. You can build castles in Spain, steal the Golden Fleece, discover Atlantis, realize your childhood dreams and adult ambitions" (5). Mind-wandering here refers to literal adjustments in human consciousness that, presumably, correlate directly with altered brain states as measurable as the unrecorded alpha waves in Guy Debord's frontal lobes as, some 30 years earlier, he drifted through Paris as a founding member of the Situationist International. Readers, too, embark on inward journeys, even unknowingly, as we follow Joseph Conrad's Kurtz or Marlow as they slip into the heart of darkness.[7]

Reading counts among our most important brain-based, mind-wandering activities, and it remains a deep mystery why its neurology remains so neglected in literary studies.[8] Michael C. Corballis, a psychologist, offers a nontechnical introduction to the mind's built-in capacity to slip away. In *The Wandering Mind: What the Brain Does When You're Not Looking* (2015), he proposes that detective stories, for example, initiate "an exercise in guided mind-wandering, escorting us into different places, different times, different minds."[9] The digital humanities, if well integrated with neuroscience, may one day provide insights into mind-wandering as intrinsic to reading—not a dereliction of readerly duties—perhaps tracing multibranched neural pathways as distinctive as our fingerprints.[10] At the moment, it is more useful to take (as philosophers sometimes say) a step back.

Digression (from Latin, "to step aside") offers a specific instance of mind-wandering that stamps texts with a distinctive formal signature. Xavier de Maistre, born into an aristocratic European family, in his late 20s finds himself confined for six weeks under house arrest. With nowhere to go, he wanders indoors, composing an odd nonfiction narrative entitled, in literal English translation, *Voyage Around My Room* (1794). The word *voyage* (from Latin *via*, meaning "way" or "route") refers to journeys in general, not just by ship, but de Maistre hijacks its nautical sense to enrich the ironies of an expedition undertaken in a landlocked room 36 paces in perimeter. Moreover, he infuses this rectangular space with impromptu diversions and curved trajectories that reflect his disdain for straightforward narrative progressions. Instead, he aims to follow his own whims and fancies, "without keeping to any one course."[11] The result is a wily text that takes readers on a mind-wandering drift through a material space that doubles as the inner space of de Maistre's idiosyncratic psyche.

Mind-wandering in the company of Xavier de Maistre is entirely unpredictable, proceeding through fragments, glimpses, quick cuts, and fugitive movements, with no straining after high seriousness, general truths, or even order. What he offers instead is the Montaigne-like portrait of a mind in motion that leaves any settled path behind. "I shall even zigzag this way and that, and follow every line possible in geometry, if necessary," he writes (8). The armchair, for example, sparks a reverie about long winter evenings by the fire. Then, heading north from the armchair, he meets his bed, and beds too inspire the psychic drift into a new cache of mind-wandering treasures. De Maistre, in his mental travel, improvises an escape from the binary trap of going somewhere or going nowhere. *Going* is not an issue. The issue, for seriocomic mind-wandering, is play: the entry into a child-like condition free from adult supervision and deeply transgressive in its dreamlike and pleasure-centered experience of pure being.

The literary master of digression is Laurence Sterne—enormously popular in France as in England—who also provides inspiration for de Maistre. The Life and Opinions of Tristram Shandy, Gentleman, published in nine volumes between 1759 and 1767, is a daring, high-wire performance in which the novel (Tristram's purported autobiography) not only departs from straightforward narrative chronologies but also merges with Sterne's authorial whims, quirks, and dizzying improvisations. He once offers readers a supposedly helpful guide to the shape of the narrative, with four layers of squiggles, loops, prongs, and visual hiccups.[12] Tristram Shandy is less about fidelity to the facts of Tristram's life—the ostensible subject—than about fidelity to a mind-wandering consciousness that ambiguously fuses the voices of character and author. There is enough mind-wandering in Tristram Shandy to set off alpha waves all across Western Europe.

Sterne and Xavier de Maistre establish a pedigree for subsequent writers who seek to disrupt readerly conventions and tap into the possibilities of active mind-wandering. They also establish the playful, game-like aura that appeals to certain experimental contemporary writers. Georges Perec, for example, pursues a rule-breaking set of new rules ultimately designed to disrupt the conventional readerly filters that actively discourage or prevent mind-wandering. In "Species of Spaces" (1974), for example, Perec arbitrarily shrinks his range to the bed, bedroom, door, wall, and other nearby structures; much like de Maistre, he encourages the mind to wander in ways that recover a lost realm of consciousness. On staircases: "We don't think enough about staircases."[13] Earlier he had composed an entire book—La Disparition (1969)—excluding any word that contains the letter *e*, an arbitrary device that opens up a world that excludes the French words for mother, father, brother, sister, water, earth, and sky. We must wander elsewhere. Such fictive games bore some readers, although on occasion they have returned with insightful apologies for too-quick dismissals.[14] What matters most is that mind-wandering operates in multiple registers, literary and personal, and we ignore its importance at our loss, since it reflects or re-opens the world in which we spend 50% or more of our lives. Reading and mind-wandering are different actions, but they share a deep kinship, and (like minds and bodies) they proceed together.

Mind-wandering, as bibliophiles know, can reach an apex of pleasure as book lovers drift among bookcases stacked high with unopened treasures. It also helps Jean-Dominique Bauby complete the astonishing memoir that appears two days before his death, becoming an instant bestseller.

Notes

1 The Oxford Handbook of Spontaneous Thought: Mind-Wandering, Creativity, and Dreaming, ed. Kieran C. R. Fox and Kalina Christoff (New York: Oxford University Press, 2018).

2 See, for example, Antonio R. Damasio, Descartes' Error: Emotion, Reason and the Human Brain (New York: Putnam, 1994); George Lakoff and Mark Johnson, Metaphors We Live By (1980; rpt. Chicago: University of Chicago Press, 2003).

3 William Wordsworth, "I Wandered Lonely as a Cloud" (1807), in The Collected Poems of William Wordsworth (Ware, Hertfordshire: Wordsworth Editions Limited, 1992), ll.19–22.

4 See Timothy D. Wilson, Strangers to Ourselves: Discovering the Adaptive Unconscious (Cambridge: Harvard University Press, 2002).

5 Jean-Dominique Bauby, The Diving Bell and the Butterfly: A Memoir of Life in Death, trans. Jeremy Leggatt (New York: Vintage Books, 1997), 103. The book was published in French in the same year: 1997. Further quotations are documented within the text.

6 Alison Escalante, "New Science: Why Our Brains Spend 50% of the Time Mind-Wandering," *Forbes*, 28 January 2021, https://www.forbes.com/sites/alisonescalante/2021/01/28/new-science-why-our-brains-spend-50-of-the-time-mind-wandering.

7 Eric J. Leed, The Mind of the Traveler: From Gilgamesh to Global Tourism (New York: Basic Books, 1991).
8 See David B. Morris, "Reading Is Always Biocultural," *New Literary History* 37, no. 3 (2006): 539–561.
9 Michael C. Corballis, The Wandering Mind: What the Brain Does When You're Not Looking (Chicago: University of Chicago Press, 2015), 104. See also Georges Poulet, "Phenomenology of Reading," *New Literary History* 1, no. 1 (1969): 53–68; and Wolfgang Iser, "The Reading Process: A Phenomenological Approach," *New Literary History* 3, no. 2 (1972): 279–299.
10 Sarah Kenderdine, "Embodiment, Entanglement, and Immersion in Digital Cultural Heritage," in A New Companion to Digital Humanities, ed. Susan Schreibman, Ray Siemens, and John Unsworth (New York: Wiley Blackwell, 2016), 22–41; and George P. Landow, Hypertext 3.0: Critical Theory and New Media in an Era of Globalization (Baltimore, MD: Johns Hopkins University Press, 2006). The first edition appeared in 1992; Hypertext 3.0 is a revised version of the second edition, Hypertext 2.0 (1997).
11 Xavier de Maistre, Voyage Around My Room (1794), trans. Stephen Sartarelli (1994; rpt. New York: New Directions, 2016), 8.
12 Laurence Sterne, Tristram Shandy, ed. Howard Anderson (New York: Norton, 1980), 333 (vol. 6, chapter xl).
13 Georges Perec, "Species of Spaces," in Species of Spaces and Other Pieces, ed. and trans. John Sturrock, revised edn (New York: Penguin, 1999), 38.
14 Darran Anderson, "Spoken in Jest: On the Lasting Importance of Georges Perec," *3:AM Magazine*, 23 August 2020, https://www.3ammagazine.com/3am/spoken-in-jest-on-the-lasting-importance-of-georges-perec/.

11 Romantic wandering

"I wandered lonely as a cloud." This plain statement ranks among the most famous opening lines in Romantic poetry—maybe in world poetry—right up there with "Tyger Tyger, burning bright." The speaker's lonely cloud-like wandering in Wordsworth's poem is not a steady state but rather the significant prelude to a sudden interruption:

> When all at once I saw a crowd,
> A host, of golden daffodils;
> Beside the lake, beneath the trees,
> Fluttering and dancing in the breeze.[1]

The singleness of the speaker contrasts with the "crowd" or "host" of flowers—also not in a steady state but wildly in motion, fluttering and dancing, a daffodil tempest so stunning that it is easy to forget what initiated the show-stopping display: a solitary, lonely act of wandering.

Wandering has a long, changing history of relations to solitude. Romantic writers infuse both solitude and wandering with new significance. Solitude comes to embrace emotional experiences ranging from social isolation to cosmic interconnection, while wandering thrusts forth almost a new cast of characters all named, obliquely if not openly, the Wanderer. While it is possible to wander as a group or even as an entire people, like the Israelites following Moses into the desert, Romantic wanderers are most often singular, solitary figures. If by accident two singular wanderers meet, they will most likely wander off again, separately, in opposite directions.

Wordsworth's distinctive contribution to Romantic wandering includes a focus—as when he stumbles upon the fluttering daffodils—on accident. That is, the solitary wanderer embodies a crucial openness to the unexpected. Preceding writers on aesthetics had thoroughly staked out expectations as to where readers or travelers could encounter the sublime and beautiful, whether in Homer and Milton or in

DOI: 10.4324/9781003255307-11

rugged, wild landscapes and seascapes: aesthetic surrogates of mountain gloom and mountain glory. Wordsworth's speaker not only wanders into an *explosion* of wildflowers: the wildflowers are also totally commonplace—garden-variety daffodils—the homely opposite of the sublime and beautiful.

Wandering for Wordsworth is what guarantees encounters with the unexpected that trigger improvised acts of the imagination. Coleridge recalls that while working together on Lyrical Ballads he and Wordsworth compared the transforming power of imagination to a familiar landscape suddenly altered by "accidents of light and shade."[2] *Accidents* is the key word: what wandering offers is the unforeseen and the unplanned, chance events that, as it were, just happen. You might just happen to wander into a scene of dancing, fluttering daffodils that strikes you with the power of an epiphany.

Emerging as newly prominent figures in the nineteenth-century cultural landscape, wanderers certainly reflect political and economic changes that permit tourists to travel in search of experiences previously restricted to aristocrats on the Grand Tour. Wordsworth's Guide to the Lakes (1810), often reprinted, is not exactly a handbook for wanderers, but many travelers consulted it, especially looking for landscapes that might remind them of paintings. These so-called picturesque travelers often carried a Claude glass: handheld mirror-like devices designed to enhance landscape views. Significantly, the crucial move in operating a Claude glass is to turn your back on nature. Then, with the desired landscape scene behind, you raise the Claude glass to shoulder level and gaze into the convex surface. As if by magic, the scene reflected in the glass resembles a landscape painting by Claude Lorrain. On the hunt for outdoor paintings in all the old familiar places, picturesque travelers in effect rule out accidents.

Wandering, in its openness to the accidental, without expectations and minus a Claude glass, confronts Wordsworth's speaker with more than dancing daffodils. It is a host, a sudden uncountable profusion: "ten thousand saw I at a glance." *Ten thousand* is a poetic equivalent of infinity or countlessness, like the stars in Carl Sagan's trademark phrase *billions and billions*. Wordsworth's wanderer sees daffodils everywhere, beneath the trees, beside the lake. The vision is less like the static image in a Claude glass than like an animated film. It appears, moreover, all at once, in a single glance, as if a profusion of stars erupted, all at once, to fill a totally black night sky. You might be lucky enough to see it—almost by accident—but only if you wander.

Wordsworth's daffodils hold one more resonance. Daffodils bloom in the very early spring, as Shakespeare notes. The Winter's Tale includes a weather-wise appreciation of daffodils that "come before the swallow dares, and take/ The winds of March with beauty" (IV.iv). March, as British wanderers know, marks a muddy transition, an uncertain tipping point, with winter in retreat but spring not yet fully arrived. The cold, blustery winds are what send the daffodils into wild motion. March, not April, may be the cruelest month, when daffodils add a golden beauty to the winter-stunted, storm-soaked soil.

Wordsworth rarely stops wandering. He covers some 175,000 miles on foot during his lifetime, according to Thomas De Quincey. He composes his poems while walking, preferably (as Coleridge reports) "walking up and down a straight gravel-walk, or in some spot where the continuity of his verse met with no collateral interruption."[3] William Hazlitt rightly observed that Wordsworth's thoughts are his real subjects. His thoughts, however, are mostly rooted in specific places and in particular natural facts, almost retrospective mini-psychogeographies, as suggested by the full title of a poem usually known only in its shorthand version: "Lines Composed a Few Miles above Tintern Abbey, On Revisiting the Banks of the Wye during a Tour, July 13, 1798." (Tours today, often run by giant internet travel firms, opt for pithier mottos like—this is actual—*wander wisely*.)

"Tintern Abbey" embodies a doubleness typical of Wordsworth's wandering. Two visions are at issue: one present (available to the eye) and one past (available, in memory, to the "inward eye"). Wandering thus holds a double reward: the present tense sight and its past tense recollection. It is the past tense scenes ("recollected in tranquility") that for Wordsworth prove crucial, much like his memory of the daffodils flashing across his visual mind-space or inward eye, a process that he calls "the bliss of solitude":

> And then my heart with pleasure fills,
> And dances with the daffodils.

Solitude, whether he is wandering alone outdoors or remembering alone indoors, is less important here than the intense present-tense experience of "bliss." *Bliss* is the significant term, like *delight* for Blake and *joy* for Coleridge, implying an emotional response inseparable from the highest levels of imaginative perception—anchored, for Wordsworth, in his experience of the natural world. The wandering that brings him into contact with nature proves indispensable, when even daffodils can inspire wonder, and "Tintern Abbey" leaves no doubt concerning its extraordinary importance.

Postmodern Paris suited Guy Debord and the Situationists as they wandered the city streets, convinced (in their Marxist-inflected view) that cities reveal most clearly how socioeconomic systems organize human consciousness. Wordsworth chooses to organize his consciousness by wandering in nature.

It was in 1790 while a student at Cambridge that Wordsworth embarked with classmate Robert Jones on a three-month excursion across France. The Bastille had fallen just the year before. Although the well-planned trip provides an interlude from academic duties, there is nothing leisurely about it, especially given the revolutionary turmoil then transforming France. "A march it was of military speed," as Wordsworth describes it in 1805, a breakneck pace that is the kinetic antithesis of mindful or contemplative:

> Day after day, up early and down late,
> From hill to vale we dropped, from vale to hill
> Mounted—from province on to province swept,
> Keen hunters in a chase of fourteen weeks....[4]

Marching belongs to a gait or stylized movement incompatible with wandering. A tour that unfolds with "military speed" and with the single-mindedness of "hunters" chasing their prey proceeds in exact opposition to the manner of an early March wanderer suddenly encountering, as if by accident, a fluttering, astonishing profusion of wind-blown golden daffodils.

Wandering depends on movement at an unhurried pace, as if time were on holiday and left to drift, improvising a path rather than chasing a prey, embracing whatever happens or just falls out, open to commonplace, dazzling accidents of light and shade. It might be said—although with a sideward glance—that Wordsworth's entire development as a poet depended on learning how to wander.

Notes

1 William Wordsworth, "I Wandered Lonely as a Cloud" (1807), in The Collected Poems of William Wordsworth (Ware, Hertfordshire: Wordsworth Editions Limited, 1994), ll.3–6.

2 Samuel Taylor Coleridge, Biographia Literaria (1817), ed. James Engell and W. Jackson Bate (Princeton: Princeton University Press, 1983), II, 5 (Chapter 14).

3 William Hazlitt, "My First Acquaintance with Poets" (1823), in William Wordsworth: The Critical Heritage 1793–1820, ed. Robert Woof (New York: Routledge, 2001), 43.

4 William Wordsworth, The Prelude: The Four Texts (1798, 1799, 1805, 1850), ed. Jonathan Wordsworth (London: Penguin, 1995), VI.491–497. The Prelude was completed in 1805 but not published until 1850. Quotations here are from the 1850 text.

12 Travelers, tourists, and tramps

Tourists and travelers both wander at times, but what is it that distinguishes tourists from travelers? One thing, according to anthropologist Valene L. Smith: discretionary income.[1]

Income matters. The English aristocrats on the Grand Tour amid the palaces and cathedrals of Europe often possessed massive estates. Tourists today can book cruises at various price points, but discretionary income is still crucial. Travelers, by contrast, may be on a shoestring budget or well heeled, but income matters far less in identifying travelers. (Footwear seems their most distinctive trait.) Clearly, this is a flexible distinction. Individual travelers and tourists, like wanderers, come from all income brackets. The van-dwellers who inhabit nomadlands, however, mostly wander away from social systems that provide them with discretionary income, often living near subsistence levels. Discretionary income for many wanderers is conspicuous by its absence: wandering, in Smith's formula, mostly reflects a chronic *lack* of discretionary funds. Wandering is not travel and it is not tourism.

Tourism and travel today are big business. The American travel and tourism industry in 2017 generated over $1.6 trillion in economic output, supporting 7.8 million US jobs. Travel and tourism also accounted for 11% of all US exports and 32% of all US exports involving services. Much as headaches and backaches now occur within vast, overarching health care systems, even weekend getaways and annual holidays intersect, at some level, with an industrial system of travel and tourism that maintains cruise ships the size of floating apartment buildings. Like it or not, we are all consumers of travel: a relatively new industry that racks up huge profits and employs an armada of online booking companies. One such travel giant—closing its ads with the mantra *wander wisely*—deliberately seeks to enfold even wandering into their global cash nexus.

DOI: 10.4324/9781003255307-12

Wandering wisely—with the hidden subtext *buy our services*—is exactly what tourists as savvy consumers are trained to do and what actual wanderers prefer to avoid. The travel and tourism industry has little use for actual wanderers, an unpredictable (generally cash-poor) lot, much as wanderers have little use for industries, except for stopgap paying gigs. Wandering is almost predicated upon a resistance to whatever approaches industrial strength, which is perhaps why it emerges so prominently during the era of British and European Romanticism, when railroads, steam engines, gas lighting, coal mines, and steel mills signaled the start of a new era in urban and industrial development. Wandering offers a means of evading issues of gain and loss by stepping outside the frame of discretionary income so vital to the travel and tourism industry.

Samuel Taylor Coleridge, who named his first two sons after philosophers, addresses his infant son Hartley in "Frost at Midnight" (1798) with a wish that reflects a new and widespread Romantic mythology of the child. London-bred, Coleridge hopes that Hartley will escape his own childhood fate confined—his word is "pent"—in an urban environment:

> But thou, my babe! shalt wander like a breeze
> By lakes and sandy shores, beneath the crags
> Of ancient mountain, and beneath the clouds....[2]

Pent does not share the same root as *penitentiary*, but they both imply confinement. The desire that his young son will "wander like a breeze" reflects how far wandering for Coleridge has absorbed a sense of freedom: freedom from urban confinement and freedom from a confined education. He invokes Nature not as offering a menu of vacationlands in which to wander wisely but as—in its power to shape minds and spirits—the "Great universal Teacher!"

Wandering—like a breeze by lakes and sandy shores—holds quasi-erotic seductions that gain added power in relation to the increasing confinements of work and adult responsibility. It evokes childhood play and grown-up fantasies, like versions of the paradise designed so that hobos have no need for discretionary income: "Where a bum can stay for many a day/ And he don't need any money."[3] Hartley Coleridge, despite his philosophical namesake, did indeed wander off course in a rather desultory life, unlike his scholarly younger brother, Derwent, named for a river. Wandering in "Frost at Midnight" affirms the value of a natural education that can't be squeezed into a syllabus or sold in the academic marketplace. Hartley, however, like Matthew

Arnold's later scholar gypsy, also exposes the losses implicit in wandering away from cultural and industrial systems that can support as well as confine.

Most wanderers have lost something. Wandering van-dwellers have often suffered specific losses—job, income, spouse—while knights errant in the Middle Ages wander in search of a missing object: the Holy Grail or a damsel in distress. The most important losses, however, may be difficult to identify. "I long ago lost a hound, a bay horse, and a turtle-dove," Thoreau writes in Walden (1854), "and am still on their trail. Many are the travellers I have spoken [to] concerning them.... I have met one or two who had heard the hound, and the tramp of the horse, and even seen the dove disappear behind a cloud, and they seemed as anxious to recover them as if they had lost them themselves."[4] Such loss invokes a kind of vanishing point, where whatever Thoreau seeks has not quite fully disappeared. Wandering, unlike tourism, often invokes the elusive quality of a vague or symbolic good—a biblical pearl of great price—lost, but not quite wholly vanished, as if always just out of eyesight in a suspended state of almost-disappearing.

"It was difficult to reach Rilke," explains Stefan Zweig about his Austrian countryman and contemporary, poet Rainer Maria Rilke. "He had no house, no address where one could find him, no home, no steady lodging, no office," Zweig continues. "He was always on his way through the world, and no one, not even he himself, knew in advance which direction he would take." Zweig does not specifically identify Rilke as a wanderer, but his description reflects a quality of loss and near-disappearance typical of wandering, which can turn deadly serious. An immensely popular writer during the 1930s, Zweig left Austria during the rise of Hitler, traveling to England, America, and Brazil. Shortly after giving his publisher the manuscript containing his description of Rilke, Zweig committed suicide. "Thousands may have passed by this young man," he concludes, "with his slightly melancholy drooping blond mustache and his somewhat Slavic features, undistinguished by any single trait, without dreaming that this was a poet and one of the greatest of our generation...."[5] Not lost, yet impossible to find; seen but unrecognized; almost-disappearing. Wandering includes losses that occur just at the far margins of our vision.

"The Wanderer" (c. 975)—among the earliest surviving poems in English—is a primer in loss and disappearance. A later addition supplied by the Victorian Anglo-Saxonist Benjamin Thorpe, the title accurately translates the relevant Anglo-Saxon noun *eardstapa*. "The Earth-Stepper"—a literal translation—is a solitary warrior who wanders the earth after losing his warlord-and-patron, now long dead.

The Wanderer, as generations now call him, laments also the loss of his former warrior-companions. Friendless, he extends his lament to include the shortness of all human life. Nature—definitely not Coleridge's "great teacher"—holds no lessons and no solace. It is rather a cold, bleak, hostile, and inhuman terrain of loss.

The warrior code demands silence in the face of hardship. The Wanderer, unable to keep silent, laments alone, before dawn, with only seabirds to hear him. The isolation often implicit in solitary wandering is internal as well as external, and dreams intensify the pain: "then friendless he wakes again,/ sees wave-ridges before him,/ seabirds swimming, flaunting their feathers,/ frost and snow mingled with hail/ then his heart-wounds are heavier,/ sore with longing...."[6] Wandering becomes almost the sign of an existential universe given over to death: "Where has the horse gone? Where is the rider? Where has the treasure-giver gone?" The classical *ubi sunt* motif here may reflect the intrusive hand of a monkish scribe, but the frost and hail and heart-wounds infuse it with pagan fatality. Wandering occasionally in its isolation makes contact with a threadbare, almost tragic quality, as in King Lear's vision—as he wanders on the storm-tossed heath—that recognizes humans (stripped of their cultural pretensions) as poor, bare, forked animals. The treasure-giver, despite all his treasures, is gone. Not almost-disappearing. Utterly, forever, gone.

Charlie Chaplin accomplishes a rare feat when he manages—in the new visual medium of cinema—to create a seriocomic modern figure strangely representative of wandering outsiders, the Little Tramp (Figure 12.1).

Chaplin debuted the Little Tramp in 1915, describing him as "a man with a soul—a point of view." "He wears an air of romantic hunger," Chaplin adds, "forever seeking romance, but his feet won't let him."[7] The oversize shoes (exaggerating his unromantic feet) occupy a space somewhere in between clown-like excess and abject poverty. His faded gentleman's outfit—a thrift store purchase or the remnant of a better life—almost advertises vagrancy. A ragtag figure on the edges of a society that clearly rejects him, the Little Tramp embodies loss, but his efforts to keep up appearances let him rise marginally above circumstances he will never overcome. As a tramp, he belongs to a down-and-out confederacy that includes hobos and bums, but with a subtle difference. As a standard quip goes: "The hobo works and wanders, the tramp drinks and wanders, and the bum just drinks." *Hobo*, slang for an unemployed and homeless man, first appears following the Civil War, and hobos tend to reappear after major downturns in local and

Figure 12.1 Charlie Chaplin. Promotional photo for *The Tramp* (1915). From the archives of Roy Export Co., Ltd.

national economies, even achieving a certain distinction as a semiorganized body.[8] (The Hobo National Convention in 1889 publishes a 15-point Hobo Ethical Code.) Chaplin's Little Tramp, like the hobo, engenders a limited sympathy for living a self-reliant and mostly honest, ethical existence on the margins of a social order that he cannot, by any effort of mind or will, rejoin.

Loss cannot entirely escape the shadow of mortality, but amid the deprivations of down-and-out, wandering lives, the precarious experience of loss occasionally gives rise to revelations of human endurance in the face of extreme hardship or suffering. The Wanderer in his extended lament as a lord-bereft, solitary exile embodies at least the endurance of outsiders who, like the Little Tramp in the mute space of silent film, not only cannot manage to escape their loss and solitude but also know deep in their bones that they never will escape.

Notes

1 Valene L. Smith, "Introduction," in Hosts and Guests: The Anthropology of Tourism, ed. Valene L. Smith, 2nd edn (Philadelphia: University of Pennsylvania Press, 1989), 2.
2 Samuel Taylor Coleridge, "Frost at Midnight," in The Complete Poems, ed. William Keach (New York: Penguin, 1997), ll.4–6.
3 "Big Rock Candy Mountain," first recorded by Harry "Haywire Mac" McClintock in 1928, https://mainlynorfolk.info/folk/songs/bigrockcandymountain.html.
4 Henry David Thoreau, Walden (1854), ed. Jeffrey S. Cramer (New Haven, CT: Yale University Press, 2004), 16. For a discussion of the famously ambiguous passage, see Henrik Otterberg, Hound, Bay Horse, and Turtle-Dove: Obscurity and Authority in Thoreau's Walden (Gothenburg: University of Gothenburg Press, 2005).
5 Stefan Zweig, The World of Yesterday (1942), trans. Benjamin W. Huebsch and Helmut Ripperger (1943; rpt. Lincoln: University of Nebraska Press, 1964), 141–142.
6 "The Wanderer" is preserved in a late tenth-century collection called the Exeter Book. The literal translation of the text is mine.
7 Charlie Chaplin, "A Comedian Sees the World" (1933–1934), in A Comedian Sees the World, ed. Lisa Stein Haven (Columbia: University of Missouri Press, 2014), 91.
8 See Todd DePastino, Citizen Hobo: How a Century of Homelessness Shaped America (Chicago: University of Chicago Press, 2003).

13 The art of drifting

Gertrude Stein moved to Paris in 1903 and stayed until her death in 1946. "Paris," she writes, "was where the twentieth century was."[1] Paris is also where wandering, a few decades earlier, helped invent a distinctive new urban figure who came to represent the transition to modernity: the *flâneur*.

The *flâneur*, a well-dressed urban male, might be considered the direct opposite of disreputable gypsies or bohemians. "For a long time," began an 1864 circular from the Ministry of Interior, "the government has occupied itself with guaranteeing the safety of our population against the crimes and the depredations of bands of individual vagabonds and nomads known under the name of *Bohemians*…."[2] Gypsies wandered through the countryside, with their traditional lifestyle increasingly unwelcome to the authorities. The *flâneur*, by contrast, is a respectable citizen and representative of modernity as symbolized by Paris as the city feels its way to becoming the capital of the modern world.

Wandering as a modern urban pastime is an invention of the nineteenth-century *flâneur*. The city—Paris in particular—is far more than an incidental or accidental force in the rise of the *flâneur*. Paris in the mid-nineteenth century begins to fill with new crowds of immigrants not only from rural areas of France but also from villages and cities across Western Europe, Eastern Europe, and Russia. The urban crowd thus creates a natural habitat for the *flâneur*, who (in Baudelaire's influential description) feels at home "in the heart of the multitude." While the urban multitude provides the foreground, this well-dressed figure assumes his background role as detached observer, and his semi-concealed position in the heart of the multitude allows him the added value of a self-protective anonymity. He observes the urban life swirling around him while, as Baudelaire continues, remaining "hidden from the world."[3]

DOI: 10.4324/9781003255307-13

The *flâneur*'s detached position in the midst of the crowd adds two distinctive nuances to the tradition of wandering. It is both a pursuit of the well-to-do citizen and a pursuit that unfolds with a curious new leisurely, static quality, as if it were now possible to wander motionlessly.

Wandering in place or motionlessly is an oxymoron only within a premodern concept of wandering as necessarily nomadic. The *flâneur*, in effect, remains stationary as the city swirls around him. As wanderer, he shifts the burden of motion onto the crowd and simply changes his observation post from time to time. The modern city is in perpetual motion—New York renames itself the City that Never Sleeps—and the *flâneur* stakes out his role as a connoisseur of urban moving parts. His preferred object of vision, however, is less the boulevards and buildings than the constantly flowing crowd.

The object of vision changes decisively from 1853 to 1870 when Georges-Eugène Haussmann undertakes a massive reconstruction of Paris with the directive to introduce light, air, order, and cleanliness. Within two decades, a dark medieval warren of narrow streets reemerges as a sunlit city of green parks and wide boulevards. At night, 15,000 gas-fueled streetlamps create a romantic City of Lights, while a modern underground infrastructure provides water pipes and a sewage system. City planning could serve two masters: wide boulevards permit easier troop deployments in a capital notorious for its mutinous past. The dazzling new city almost demanded someone strategically placed to admire it. The *flâneur*, already wandering in place, was just right for the job.

The *flâneur*'s semi-detached position at the heart of the multitudinous city has less to do with Romantic traditions of rural or poetic loneliness than with urban solitude as a mode of spectatorship. A sketch by Honoré Daumier (Figure 13.1) suggests how far the position of spectator is a central function of the solitary *flâneur*.

Romantic loneliness—as in the Wordsworthian poet who wanders "lonely as a cloud"—implies an almost spiritual communion with nature, a so-called natural supernaturalism, so that the solitary individual remains connected with a larger cosmic realm. The *flâneur*, while never veering toward working-class alienation, maintains a separation crucial to his role as a detached observer whose solitude embodies the new cosmopolitan spirit of independent self-regard. The *flâneur* embodies the structural separation of a mirror in which the city both admires and comes to recognize itself.

Wandering, as the *flâneur* shifts his locales, is predominantly a male privilege. *Flâneur* derives from an Old Norse infinitive that means "to

Figure 13.1 After Honoré Daumier. *Le Flâneur.* Illustration from Louis Huart, Physiologie du flâneur (1841). Screenshot.

wander with no purpose." Although it is hard to imagine Vikings wandering around with no purpose, it is easy to picture them as male. The French knew how to improve an Old Norse verb, turning it to imply both a refined sensibility and an upper-class male privilege. Amantine Dupin did stroll the Paris streets, but, significantly, she strolled in men's clothing, much as she published under the pen name George Sand. Women wandering the streets of Paris alone were likely servants, shopkeepers, or prostitutes—or taken for such.[4] The *flâneur* didn't just happen to be male. His gender is as constitutive of *flâneur*-ship as his sensibility and attire. He embodies a form of urban wandering reserved for upper-class male representatives of the fashionable new capital city and of the emerging world of capital.

The *flâneur*, unlike Paris, failed to survive the new world of mechanized trench warfare. Walter Benjamin, soon trapped and lost in the jaws of World War II, describes a new urban figure who replaces the *flâneur* and better reflects the catastrophic postwar era: the ragpicker. As a collector of waste and debris, the ragpicker embodied Benjamin's critique of urban life under capitalism.[5] Just as modern cities continuously change, however, the ragpicker eventually disappears along with the *flâneur*. One function they both shared nonetheless remains constant: the changing modern city, as if inherently self-reflexive, periodically thrusts forth a new and distinctive figure who both observes and represents it—through the act of wandering. Wandering, as it embodies its changing roles of urban self-observation, necessarily also changes its style and performance.

Wandering, as necessary rather than incidental to the process of observing, eventually requires a style commensurate with the vast size and continual motion of the city under observation. An immobile stance is limited and inherently flawed. *The New Yorker* magazine, for example, in 1925 introduces readers of its inaugural issue to a feature entitled "The Talk of the Town." Contributing writers E. B. White and James Thurber soon make it famous for bemused verbal snapshots of city life, and their apt observations proceed as if from an unnamed wandering spectator. William Shawn, who for several decades edited "The Talk of the Town," called it "the soul of the magazine." It required from its writers, he notes, "a sensitiveness to the particulars of place, situation, and event."[6] That is, it no longer requires an *actual* wanderer but rather a wandering *viewpoint*: semi-concealed but hypersensitive to the ubiquitous flow of city life.

Urban wandering, as it shifts back to Paris, gives rise once again to a new generation of urban collective observers. Writer and theorist Guy Debord takes Paris as the focus for a quasi-scientific investigation of how cities as spatial environments organize human consciousness, emotion, and behavior. His project attracts various loosely affiliated artists and left-wingers who together take the name Situationists. From the group's founding in 1957 until its dissolution in 1972, the Situationists practice what Debord (with a theorist's flair for terminology) calls psychogeography.

Any lingering academic stiffness in the term psychogeography the Situationists undercut with a Dadaist spirit of play, so as not to be mistaken for (ultra-serious) phenomenologists. They also pursue a leftist critique that views capitalist ideologies as a primary force organizing how we act, feel, and think. As a creation and home of capital, Paris offers a perfect venue for study, and in practice the Situationist method is simply to wander, less as spectators of the city than as spectators of their own city-inflected consciousness. They add, however, one distinctive provision. Ideal urban wandering deliberately proceeds in an unfocused, oneiric state they call *la dérive.*[7]

La dérive maintains close contact with dream (*le rêve*) and with reverie (*la rêverie*). As in a daydream, it implies a letting go, a suspension of choice in favor of meandering impulses. Drift, as Debord recommends it, opens the mind to an unregulated flow of whatever chance, memory, and the environment offer. What Paris offers, in Debord's developing view, is a society spellbound by images and by image-bearing commodities. The Society of the Spectacle, his groundbreaking book published in 1967, argues that social life is no longer experienced directly or *immediately* but only indirectly, as it is *mediated* by images. The exponential rise of television, the internet, and social media support a view that consciousness is dominated today by images and by their three-dimensional replicas, from Disneyland animatronics to celebrity lookalikes. Wandering, in the era of digital reproduction, cannot escape a commodity-driven immersion in images and *simulacra.* We not only wander now through an electronic hall of mirrors. We wander, even if immovably in front of a screen, through a mobile universe of images that, as Debord recognized, inescapably shape and alter the wanderers.

The French Situationists in their dreamlike urban wandering—described by a caustic British journalist as "middle-aged men in Gore-Tex"—proved inadvertently that human consciousness even in a state of drift or *dérive* possesses powerful filters that leave portions of the urban environment invisible.[8] Lauren Elkin in Flâneuse (2016) describes research that takes her from Tokyo and Venice to Paris and New York tracking modern women travelers and writers who, in effect, reinvent the possibilities of female urban experience. Walking proves central to her story, although she does not distinguish sharply between walking and wandering. Most studies of walking, however, as Elkin observes, leave out a woman's experience and point of view, and so too for wandering. Male travel writers, for example, often do not take into account or recognize the women around them, as if the women are invisible. Even *la dérive*, whatever insights it may provide about human consciousness, cannot easily avoid the distorted, gender-inflected images surrounding us daily.

Elkin proceeds to set the record straight. The unseen female urban walker has a material presence as real and consequential as any attributed to her better-known male urban counterparts, from the *flâneur* to the psychogeographer, with perhaps a crucial exception: she does not fully share their semi-detached spectatorship. "She is going somewhere or coming from somewhere; she is saturated with in-betweenness," as

Elkin writes. "She may be a writer, or she may be an artist, or she may be a secretary or an au pair. She may be unemployed. She may be unemployable. She may be a wife or a mother, or she may be totally free. She may take the bus or the train when she's tired. But mostly, she goes on foot. She gets to know the city by wandering its streets...."[9]

Notes

1 Gertrude Stein, Paris France (New York: Charles Scribner's Sons, 1940), 11.
2 Quoted in Becky Taylor, Another Darkness, Another Dawn: A History of Gypsies, Roma and Travellers (London: Reaktion Books, 2014), 131.
3 Charles Baudelaire, "The Painter of Modern Life" (1863), in The Painter of Modern Life and Other Essays, trans. and ed. Jonathan Mayne (New York: Phaidon, 1964), 9.
4 Rebecca Solnit, Wanderlust: A History of Walking (New York: Viking Penguin, 2000), 234. See also Lauren Elkin, Flâneuse: Women Walk the City in Paris, New York, Tokyo, Venice, and London (New York: Farrar, Straus and Giroux, 2016).
5 Walter Benjamin, "Paris, the Capital of the Nineteenth Century," in Selected Writings, trans. Edmund Jephcott, Howard Eiland, and Others, ed. Howard Eiland and Michael W. Jennings, 4 vols., III (Cambridge: Harvard University Press, 2002), 32–49; and The Arcades Project, trans. Howard Eiland and Kevin McLaughlin (Cambridge: Harvard University Press, 1999). Benjamin wrote "Paris, the Capital of the Nineteenth Century" twice, in 1935 and 1939, both preliminary studies for the unfinished Arcades Project.
6 Quoted in Lillian Ross, "Editor's Preface," in The Fun of It: Stories from the Talk of the Town, ed. Lillian Ross (New York: Modern Library, 2001), xviii, xvii.
7 See Guy Debord, "Theory of the *Dérive*" (1958), in Situationist International Anthology, ed. and trans. Ken Knabb, revised edn (Berkeley: Bureau of Public Secrets, 2006), 62–66; and *Situationist International Online*, https://www.cddc.vt.edu/sionline/si/situ.html.
8 Will Self, Psychogeography: Disentangling the Modern Conundrum of Psyche and Place (New York: Bloomsbury USA, 2007), 12. I owe this reference to Lauren Elkin.
9 Elkin, Flâneuse, 22. See also Janet Wolff, "The Invisible Flâneuse: Women and the Literature of Modernity, Theory, Culture and Society 2, no. 3 (1985): 37–46.

14 The Wandering Jew

Yahweh is angry: "And the LORD's anger was kindled against Israel and he made them wander in the wilderness forty years, until all the generation, that had done evil in the sight of the LORD, was consumed."[1]

Wandering holds a significant place in biblical history beginning with Cain, and the wanderers quickly accumulate. It is the Israelites—the 12 tribes descended from Abraham—who next resume wandering, once again as a divine punishment. Moses, after freeing the Israelites from bondage in Egypt, leads them not to the Promised Land but straight into the wilderness. They wander there for the next 40 years.

Yahweh intends the 40-year desert wandering not only as punishment but also as the slow-motion replacement of an entire generation. Wandering allows a rupture with the status quo. It clears space for a new beginning. The Israelites who embark on their desert punishment still bear their former slave mentalities, but over 40 years a new generation is born, both free from bondage and untainted by slavery. Moses and his brother Aaron in effect set up a roving desert seminar: a crash course on freedom and self-rule, which includes the laws brought back from Mt. Sinai. Paulo Freire in Pedagogy of the Oppressed (1968) describes the reeducation needed in order for all oppressed peoples, once unchained, to embrace a freedom that does not simply replicate the abusive power of their oppressors, which is the only power they have known.

Wandering is closely aligned with ideologies of freedom, and liberation movements often find their inspiration, model, and metaphors in the Israelite escape from bondage. Such freedom, while enjoyed as a personal endowment, depends on the liberation of an entire people. Walt Whitman in his "Poem of The Road" (1856) speaks both

DOI: 10.4324/9781003255307-14

personally and as the self-appointed wandering representative of a new democratic order:

> From this hour, freedom!
> From this hour, I ordain myself loosed of limits
> and imaginary lines!
> Going where I list—my own master, total and absolute....[2]

Freedom and self-mastery, alas, rarely constitute a rainbow arc stretching directly from bondage to liberation. Freedom for one group may mean that another group faces oppression, much as European settlers in North America (once free from Old World constraints) deny the same freedoms to Native American peoples. Liberation from chains and slavery may lead to social prejudice and psychological oppression equally onerous. Jews, as descendants of the wandering Israelites, soon face new displacements and oppression. Diasporas, pogroms, ghettos, and anti-Semitism all testify to the punishing repressions that the medieval Christian and Muslim worlds imposed upon Jews as designated wandering Outsiders.

Jewish otherness—as a quality assigned by non-Jews—found a striking historical symbol in a primal figure who comes to stand as the punitive stereotype of an entire (unfree) people: the Wandering Jew.[3]

The Wandering Jew, as the creation of international anti-Semitism, compresses in a single figure toxic themes of exile and otherness. The story begins with a dubious biblical claim from the Gospel of John. As Jesus drags his cross to the Crucifixion, he asks to rest on the bench outside the shop of a Jewish shoemaker. The shoemaker refuses and Jesus replies with cryptic wordplay on rest and restlessness, which later exegetes interpret as a curse. The upshot is a biblical tradition in which the shoemaker, as punishment for denying the Savior a temporary rest, is cursed to a life of restless wandering.

The crucial Cain-like addendum? The shoemaker will wander ceaselessly, until the end of time. He becomes another archetype of the eternal wanderer.

The shoemaker has a Latin name, Ahasuerus, and he remains a staple of popular religious literature from the Middle Ages on. A seventeenth-century broadside details his fate as an eternal wanderer in ragged verse meant for wide distribution among the semiliterate faithful:

> No Resting could he find at all,
> no Ease or Heart's Content,

No House, no Home, no Dwelling-place;
  but wandring forth he went,
From Town to Town, in Foreign Lands,
  with grieved Conscience still,
Repenting for the hanious Guilt
  of his fore-passed Ill.[4]

The scant biblical authority is hardly enough to explain the enduring popularity of the legend—without anti-Semitism. Although depictions of outsiders between 1660 and 1830 often reflect an anti-Semitic bias, extreme prejudice against Jews as outsiders easily melds with the long, dark history of political hate.[5] A 1940 Nazi propaganda film is titled, as if obvious, *The Eternal Jew (Der ewige Jude)*.

Marc Chagall, born Moishe Zakharovich Shagal to Jewish parents in Belarus, paints a version of the Wandering Jew that reflects both the enduring power of the legend and its possibilities for Jewish reinterpretation. He painted it just after his return to Paris in 1925, which had been interrupted by World War I. The war killed over 13 million civilians and some 8.5 million military, leaving Europe still haunted less than a decade after its official end in 1918. The war had also displaced over one million Jews and destroyed the last remnants of peasant-based *shtetl* culture that for centuries had sustained East European Jewish life. In World War II, six million Jews died in the Holocaust. Significantly, Chagall's *Wandering Jew* (Figure 14.1) does not resemble a curse-bearing scapegoat but appears more like a sturdy, resilient peasant out of Yiddish folklore.

Chagall's Wandering Jew, while impossible to separate from a brutal war and killing Holocaust, emerges as a figure whose endless wandering may be also seen as a testament to Jewish survival.

The painting repays a closer look. The figure of Ahasver (no longer the Latinate Ahasuerus) occupies the entire foreground and fills much of the picture space. As if sprung from the earth, he strides forward pressed close to the road or soil, earthbound, wrapped in thick, coarse, cheap cloth layered against the cold like his wiry, full beard. The traditional anti-Semitic outsider remains an outsider—separated from the town behind him—but his resolute appearance betrays no fear of the road. His prominent boots look rugged enough for any crisis, his pack well provisioned, the thick walking stick a match in sheer ruggedness for the boots. This is not a figure absorbed in loss and melancholy. He appears rather, in his wandering stride, indomitable.

Chagall, a secular Jew, represents Ahasver as a figure unconstrained by his outsider status. If his position outside the town reflects this

Figure 14.1 Marc Chagall. *Ahasver, the legendary figure of the eternally wandering Jew.* Petit Palais, Musée d'Art Moderne, Geneva. Erich Lessing/Art Resource, NY.

outsider status, the town appears to include both a church and a synagogue, as did Chagall's hometown Vitebsk, where Jews and Christians lived in relative peace. His parents' house overlooked the local church.

Chagall lived on the road. As a painter, he led a wandering existence that took him from a Russian village to Paris, Saint Petersburg, Moscow, Berlin, Amsterdam, Rome, Barcelona, Cairo, Jerusalem, Tel Aviv, and New York, among other stops. "I have no place of my own...," he once observed. Then he joked, suggesting he resembled the figures in his work who seem suspended in mid-air: "I have to live someplace."[6] The Wandering Jew in Chagall's painting clearly has no fixed domicile. Wanderers have to live someplace, however temporarily, even if the lack of a settled home can feel a bit like living suspended in mid-air. In compensation, there is also a Whitmanesque sense of freedom in going where you wish, when you wish, your own master, even though such freedom (for wanderers) is never total and absolute.

Any sense of optimism raised by Chagall's portrait of human resilience and survival, however, must also recognize contrary intimations. Ahasver's warm fur hat betrays scattered spots of red, blotches or stains of ruddy color, as do his rucksack, tunic, trousers, and boots. Are they no more than painterly grace notes meant to brighten the general dark earth tones? Or do they evoke memories of blood? Memories impossible to dissociate from a catastrophic war that decimated Jewish communities? There are ineradicable costs inseparable from the full reckoning of an ongoing structural anti-Semitism that, for centuries, has cast Jews as wandering outsiders. For Jews, as Chagall shows, wandering is no sure road to freedom and no safe refuge.

Notes

1 Numbers 32:13. This quotation is from the King James Version (1611).

2 Walt Whitman, "Poem of The Road," in Leaves of Grass (1856 edn), https://whitmanarchive.org/published/LG/1856/poems/12.

3 See George K. Anderson, The Legend of the Wandering Jew (1965; rpt. Providence: Brown University Press, 1970).

4 The Wandering Jew: or The Shooemaker [sic] of Jerusalem... (London [1688–1709?]), http://ebba.english.ucsb.edu/ballad/33903/transcription.

5 See Frank Felsenstein, Anti-Semitic Stereotypes: A Paradigm of Otherness in English Popular Culture, 1660–1830 (Baltimore, MD: Johns Hopkins University Press, 1995).

6 Quoted in Richard I. Cohen, "The 'Wandering Jew' from Medieval Legend to Modern Metaphor," in The Art of Being Jewish in Modern Times, ed. Barbara Kirshenblatt-Gimblett and Jonathan Karp (Philadelphia: University of Pennsylvania Press, 2008), 173.

15 Women who wander

Does wandering take shapes or paths that match distinctive—or possibly unique—patterns of women's experience? Odysseus cannot define the single distinctive pattern that fits all male experiences of wandering, and the experience of women over many centuries is unlikely to match a single trajectory. There is no essence and no eternal mystery awaiting discovery that will define all women. Although there is a famous mythic hero's journey, there is as yet no mythic *heroine's journey*—no abstract structure or shape—only many individual journeys, plural and often unfinished, much more like wanderings than like quests.

Life-shaking trauma descended upon Cheryl Nyland in a perfect storm. Her father vanishes when she is six. Her mother, the magical center of her domestic circle, dies when Nyland is in her early 20s. As her close-knit family scatters, her marriage falls apart, or rather she tips it over a cliff while supposedly trying to save it. One-night stands and heroin find her at 26 alone in a studio apartment and working as a waitress, "as low and mixed-up as I'd ever been in my life."[1] Nyland's solution? She leaves Minneapolis to hike 1,100 miles of the Pacific Crest Trail (PCT). As she writes in her bestselling memoir Wild (2012), "I didn't know where I was going until I got there" (27).

Journeys often take the form of wandering, as for Odysseus, and wanderings often take the form of impromptu journeys. Journeys and wanderings are ambiguously interpenetrating, overlapping events. Nyland—"as mixed-up as I'd ever been"—is in a wandering state of mind. Alone, in distress, with absolutely no experience as a hiker, she is also deep within a psychic wilderness that opens up with her mother's death. In retrospect, she decides that her wild behavior in Minneapolis expressed a desire to reverse her mother's death. "The wanting," she says, "was a wilderness and I had to find my own way out of the woods" (27).

DOI: 10.4324/9781003255307-15

A hike is not exactly a journey, and hiking an established trail is not exactly wandering. Still, as experienced hikers know, even well-mapped trails branch, split, splinter, and disappear; unexpected obstacles emerge; and surplus dangers always face a woman alone hiking isolated trails for 1,100 miles. The hike, in effect, belongs to a longer journey that includes wandering. If the lines of definition are unclear, Nyland's purpose is not, and her purpose helps identify at least one important pattern of female wandering. She embarks on the PCT with, as she writes later, a single overriding desire: "to save myself" (5).

Self-rescue is distinct from the middle-class adolescent rituals of "finding oneself." The self whom Nyland seeks to save, like the self who will do the saving, is not already well established—simply awaiting rescue—but profoundly undetermined. Indeed, the woman who sets out on a mission of self-rescue is fragmented, disturbed, chaotic, and unfinished. The self whom she seeks to rescue, moreover, constitutes a new and coherent but as yet unknown self. In this confusing process of iffy, simultaneous self-rescue and self-formation, solitude and wandering perform their crucial roles of separation and of clarification. "[T]he point of my trip," she once says as she declines an offer of help, "is that I'm out here to do it alone" (122).

The female pattern of self-rescue is important in its reversal of the chivalric model in which a woman—the generic damsel in distress—passively awaits rescue by a (male) knight errant in shining armor. Nyland does not wait. She creates the self who will come to her own rescue.

The generic wanderer, in Dion DiMucci's popular song, is nameless. Self-rescue and self-formation for Nyland require self-naming. Thus, as a prelude to her hike, she initiates a divorce-inspired search for a new name, which requires abandoning her hyphenated married surname. She thinks hard and makes a list of literary options. "Nothing fit," she writes. Then, as if randomly, she encounters the adjective *strayed*—past participle of the infinitive *to stray*. She checks it in a dictionary and instantly knows it's right. "Its layered definitions spoke directly to my life," she writes, "and also struck a poetic chord: *to wander from the proper path…*" (96).

Cheryl Strayed's Wild speaks directly to many women readers, and her talents as well as her personal grit make for a compelling narrative. She is hardly responsible for how advertisers co-opt wildness and wandering. "Our Women Wanderers Tours," reads the ad for *Wild Women Travel*, "provide a venue for traveling women to journey together into exotic lands. Voyage around the globe with a supportive group of ladies that want to learn about diverse cultures and see amazing sites."[2]

Tourism, even if educational and well tailored to the specific needs of women, is exactly what Strayed's wandering journey out of her psychic wilderness is *not* about.

Legitimate questions remain about how to measure or define the act of wandering. Strayed's hike lasts for 90 days. How many days does it take to constitute a genuine act of wandering?

"How Long is the Coast of Britain?" This question is the title of an essay published in 1967 by the celebrated mathematician Benoît Mandelbrot, and the short answer is *nobody knows*. Mandelbrot's essay, now a classic in fractal geometry, yields a valuable law applicable outside geometry: any total will depend entirely on the unit of measurement. The total provided by a wooden yardstick will provide a total that differs from the total provided by a 2″ piece of string. Coastlines alter with the tide. Where does the measurement begin? At the waterline? At the dunes? As Mandelbrot observes, length will increase without limit as the scale of measurement decreases toward zero.

Wandering too is a fractal event. Does wandering change when it is a woman who wanders? Is there a unit of measurement that applies to the process of self-formation and self-rescue?

Wandering, like citizenship and landowning, was for centuries primarily a male practice. Roads and inns are dangerous places where robbers and murderers lie in wait, and women face sexual perils that men don't face. Social status also matters. Upper-class women ride in carriages protected with footmen, but beginning in the eighteenth century a few intrepid, desperate, or simply adventurous women from various social classes begin to travel alone.[3] Anne Bonny and Mary Read are even accepted into the all-male club of pirates, and they dress in men's clothing, like the few women hobos later. Women wanderers remain exceptions in the early modern era, and we know little about them, but, as Lauren Elkin argues, we need to look harder to find the women wanderers whom we simply don't expect to see.[4]

Wandering for women requires its own fractal measurements. Wives and sweethearts sometimes followed military camps, along with tradeswomen and prostitutes. The term *streetwalker* first appears in 1591, and women alone at night have faced a long history of abuse. Even among women relatively free from patriarchal constraints, it is rare to find self-described wanderers, and women who wander must somehow contend with what seem at times their nonnegotiable responsibilities as sisters, wives, and mothers, expected to run a household.[5] "Extreme domesticity," as scholar Susan Fraiman calls it, describes the arrangements that women in nontraditional, marginalized families contrive in order to provide a home-like stability.[6] Teenage runaways, sex-trafficking victims, abused spouses, military veterans, and women who are mentally ill wander out of desperation. Homeless women make people uneasy, as Stephanie Golden writes: "no category exists for a woman without family or home."[7] Anne Bonny and Mary Read are captured and sentenced to death.

Self-formation and self-rescue for Cheryl Strayed do not raise the issues of sexual identity and gender fluidity that occupy Maggie Nelson in The Argonauts (2015). Her remarkable memoir recounts the personal journey she makes together with artist Harry Dodge, born Wendy Malone, Nelson's transgender partner who is undergoing a female-to-male transition. While Dodge deals with gender changes via testosterone injections and a double mastectomy, Nelson experiences her own parallel psychic and physical changes during pregnancy: "2011, the summer of our changing bodies. Me, four months pregnant, you six months on T."[8] Her pregnancy, which propels Nelson and Dodge into the equally unfamiliar space of LGBTQ parenthood, provides the focus for Nelson's discontinuous, wandering text—alternately erudite and earthy, abstract and anecdotal—which tells the compelling story of a woman who falls in love with a woman who is in the process of becoming a male. Nelson does not describe the experience as a journey, but her title invokes the ship that carried Jason on one of the most famous wandering journeys in Greek mythology.

Nelson cites a passage by Roland Barthes about the Greek ship *Argo* that also helps explain her title. The ship undergoes a reconstruction in which every board is replaced, creating, in effect, a new ship that exactly resembles the old ship. Is it the same *Argo*? Nelson and Dodge undertake a voyage into self-replacement or self-renewal, uncertain how it will work out. Will they be the same people who began the voyage? Or are identities always in flux, gender inherently fluid? Nelson admires a feminist lecturer who, in a risky presentation, leaves an impression of being "onto something and letting us in on it before she fully understood it" (40). Nelson too is onto something, wandering into a new reality before she fully understands it, if indeed understanding is what's required.

Does anyone really understand gender? Nelson makes a point of noting Harry Dodge's "lifelong interest in fluidity and nomadism" (139). It is feminist theorist Rosi Braidotti who argues in learned detail that individuals with divergent sexual or gender identities—like other politically, racially, and culturally marginalized people—belong to the condition she calls "being nomadic."[9] Nelson's penultimate entry suggests a similar understanding as she quotes—almost as if it were a personal motto—an enigmatic passage on the nomadic order taken directly from the unofficial founding fathers of nomad theory, Gilles Deleuze and Félix Guattari: "Flying anuses, speeding vaginas, there is no castration" (143).

Deleuze and Guattari, with their surreal anuses and vaginas, refer to the unconscious as a realm of libidinal *multiplicities*. Such multiplicities, however unusual, serve as a corrective to Freud (father of the castration complex). Freud, they write, "has no understanding of multiplicities as formations of the unconscious."[10] Nelson, as she and Harry Dodge embark on their own journey of libidinal multiplicities, is less interested in self-rescue than in a writerly engagement with her own uncertainties. She seeks, in the parallel journey of writing, to understand both her experience of pregnancy and motherhood—a distinctively female pattern—and her open-ended excursion with Harry Dodge into surgery-assisted, twenty-first-century erotic terrain. Her memoir, in the discontinuous tradition of Jason's journey, ventures into ambiguously unsettled and unsettling questions. It is a prose wandering in which, as a relatively straight male reader, I am certain to get lost.

Notes

1 Cheryl Strayed, Wild: From Lost to Found on the Pacific Crest Trail (New York: Alfred A. Knopf, 2012), 5. Further quotations are documented within the text.

2 Wild Spirit Travel, https://www.wildspirittravel.com/types-of-tours/women-wanderers.

3 Ingrid Horrocks, Women Wanderers and the Writing of Mobility, 1784–1814 (Cambridge: Cambridge University Press, 2017).

4 Lauren Elkin, Flâneuse: Women Walk the City in Paris, New York, Tokyo, Venice, and London (New York: Farrar, Straus and Giroux, 2016).

5 See, for example, Joanna L. Stratton, Pioneer Woman: Voices from the Kansas Frontier (New York: Simon and Schuster, 1981); Glenda Riley, The Female Frontier: A Comparative View of Women on the Prairie and the Plains (Lawrence: University Press of Kansas, 1988); and Janet Floyd, Writing the Pioneer Woman (Columbia: University of Missouri Press, 2002).

6 Susan Fraiman, Extreme Domesticity: A View from the Margins (New York: Columbia University Press, 2017).

7 Stephanie Golden, The Women Outside: Meanings and Myths of Homelessness (Berkeley: University of California Press, 1992), 5.

8 Maggie Nelson, The Argonauts (Minneapolis, MN: Graywolf Press, 2015), 79. Further quotations are documented within the text.

9 Rosi Braidotti, Nomadic Subjects: Embodiment and Sexual Difference in Contemporary Feminist Theory (1994), 2nd edn (New York: Columbia University Press, 2011), 10.

10 Gilles Deleuze and Félix Guattari, A Thousand Plateaus: Capitalism and Schizophrenia (1980), trans. Brian Massumi (Minneapolis: University of Minnesota Press, 1987), 32.

16 Gypsy in my soul

Gypsies first appeared in Europe in the Middle Ages, as if out of nowhere. The name *gypsy* suggests an origin in Egypt, but the Romani people—as they are known today—are the descendants of an Indo-Aryan ethnic group who left India in the sixth century. Living and traveling in caravans confirmed their status as outsiders, which cast them always under suspicion, while it allowed them to scrape out a living as (reluctantly tolerated) fortune-tellers, horse traders, pedlars, and seasonal farm workers. Their otherness seemed as exotic as their black-haired, dark-eyed, swarthy features, but a wandering lifestyle also assured their reputation as cheats, petty thieves, and vagrants. Reception often turned hostile. As stateless, foreign wanderers, gypsies were once met from Western Europe to the Balkans with draconian laws and judicial persecutions that extended at times to vigilante arson and murder.[1]

Jewish otherness was contained in ghettos. The otherness of gypsies, by virtue of their wandering lifestyle, posed an implicit threat uncontainable in ghetto-like confinement. Now you see them, now you don't. They wandered off. If something is missing, it's a good bet the gypsies took it.

Gypsies—variously called Roma, Travellers, or Bohemians—no longer fit the stereotype of itinerant fortune-tellers traveling by caravan. Gypsy women no longer evoke the stereotype of smoldering, sexual, live-free-or-die firebrands such as Bizet portrayed in *Carmen* (1875). The Romani people—the name many modern gypsies prefer—today often live in small enclaves scattered from Eastern Europe to South America. Several million Romani speakers keep alive their distinctive language and dialects, including a number of families or bands living in semi-permanent settlements, often poor and rural. Roma activists have recently risen to prominence seeking social justice for an oppressed and marginalized people who have long been

DOI: 10.4324/9781003255307-16

voiceless. Justice for gypsies does not include claims on disputed territory. Gypsies may be unique among organized peoples (so journalist Isabel Fonseca suggests) in having "no dream of a homeland."[2]

Gypsies, as the Oxford English Dictionary affirms, are traditionally defined as "a wandering race," and it was their reputation as wanderers that attracted two college grads composing a song for their 1937 class reunion. "The Gypsy in My Soul," like most successful pop songs, is a little miracle of compression, and its opening lines squeeze the history of the Roma people into a cliché:

> If I am fancy free
> And love to wander
> It's just the Gypsy in my soul.[3]

The decade-long Great Depression from 1929 to 1939 at its most severe saw some 15 million Americans out of work amid a chaotic social landscape of bank failures and hobo jungles. Many Americans were not feeling particularly fancy-free. The imagined life of the Roma people, compressed into a gypsy cliché, offered a Depression-era metaphor for a fantasy of freedom.

"The Gypsy in My Soul," although evoking little more than an exotic otherness, offered radio audiences the double fantasy of wanderlust married with an emotional expressiveness. The freedom gypsies evoked was less political or social than affective. While gaily painted wagons and caravan-living helped cement the gypsy reputation for an exotic, itinerant lifestyle, their name also came to connote wild bursts of passionate feeling. Flamenco dancing originated with Andalusian gypsies in southern Spain, and the dark-haired, flashing-eyed dancers with their whirling skirts represented an unfettered ardor unavailable to hardworking bourgeois citizens struggling to pay the rent. Gypsy life thus also came to represent a mysterious, uninhibited, emotive freedom that, while associated with the allure of faraway exotic lands, corresponded directly with a yearning located deep within the self:

> There's something calling me
> From way out yonder
> It's just the Gypsy in my soul.

The "gypsy" in your soul is indirect evidence, welcome in the soul-crushing Depression, that you do indeed still possess a soul. The ultimate proof lies in your gypsy-like desire to wander.

Soul—not yet fully disconnected from theology even if secularized as the self—is something that sorely needed reaffirming, not just in 1930s America. Victorian England too had struggled with faith-shaking uncertainties as Malthus, Lyell, and Darwin introduced facts and theories that ran counter to centuries of orthodox religious conviction. Amid such soul-troubles, Matthew Arnold in 1857 received the distinguished title Oxford Professor of Poetry. He certainly deserved the honor, not only as a poet but also as a social figure ranking among the more eminent of eminent Victorians; still, his title's association with Oxford University is mildly ironic. Four years earlier, Arnold had published a long poem about a poor Oxford scholar who abandons his bookish studies to run off with a wandering band of gypsies.

Wandering is a major motif in "The Scholar-Gipsy" (1853) for reasons beyond Arnold's explanation that the poem recalls his "delightful wanderings" with a childhood friend in the Cumnor hills.[4] As Arnold depicts it, gypsy life in its itinerant otherness includes access to a secret, higher, bookless knowledge immune from the toxins of Victorian doubt. The young ex-Oxford scholar, attracted by the lure of secret knowledge, promises to publish what he learns from the gypsies, although with the proviso that he will delay writing until inspiration strikes. Inspiration as a theory of writing is among the casualties of scientific rationalism dating back to Thomas Hobbes. It stood no chance in the era of Malthus, Lyell, and Darwin, as the Oxford Professor of Poetry knew too well. The wandering scholar's long-awaited spark from heaven of course never arrives.

Wandering has a long association with error, but "The Scholar-Gipsy" does not focus on the scholar's misguided belief in divine inspiration. In fact, as a well-known man of faith, Arnold directs any critique away from the scholar and toward the doubt-shaken, tentative Victorians among whom the speaker includes himself as he addresses the stymied scholar:

> Thou waitest for the spark from heaven! and we,
> Light half-believers of our casual creeds,
> Who never deeply felt, nor clearly willed,
> Whose insight never has borne fruit in deeds,
> Whose vague resolves never have been fulfilled;
> For whom each year we see
> Breeds new beginnings, disappointments new;
> Who hesitate and falter life away,
> And lose to-morrow the ground won to-day—
> Ah! do not we, wanderer! await it too?[5]

The gypsy scholar ("wanderer!")—unlike the Victorian readers who, in effect, wander in casual unbelief—represents a life spent in seeking a higher knowledge presumably inaccessible to strictly reason-centered enterprises. His is an inherently wandering life—in spirit if not in caravans—that by virtue of its outsider status retains a gypsy-like attachment to a lost world of soul, increasingly felt to be out of reach.

Industrialist Andrew Carnegie knew Arnold personally and described him as both serious and charming: a religious man who nonetheless in a single sentence had "slain the supernatural." How do you slay the supernatural? The question concerns the validity of miracles, and Arnold, as Carnegie recalls, said that the case against miracles is closed. His one-sentence review of miracles: "They do not happen."[6]

Something in Arnold's soul, even if the door is closed to miracles, apparently still longs to hear a call from way out yonder. Gypsies—once denounced as heathens—today do not bear the burden of representing a lost world of miracle, expressiveness, and magical belief. They have begun, publicly, to assert their equal rights. Although maintaining their distinctive language and culture, they also adapt (as always) to changing social and political circumstances, including academic ways. The International Romani Union now sponsors gypsy conferences, and gypsies are emerging as spokespersons for the increasingly important global concept of transnationalism.

Gypsy lifeways, if such a generalization holds today, offer a significant insight into wandering. Wanderers almost necessarily seek out the cracks in a prevailing system. The macro-system may be a nation-state or a food industry needing migrant labor, but wanderers, like gypsies, survive in part by identifying and exploiting the cracks, even if they extend no further than lapses in local security ("every lock that ain't locked when no one's around").[7] Gypsy lifeways do not seek to dismantle systems—which would mean dismantling their own sources of livelihood—but rather to survive as outsiders adjacent to the systems they depend on: systems that cannot succeed by wholly excluding them. Doubt represents a fissure within the Victorian system of faith. "The Scholar-Gipsy" might be described as a gypsy-like poetic experiment in doubting doubt.

The Romani people (no longer drafted for double duty as metaphors) not only embody strategies of resistance to confining systems but also offer a portal to the coming transnational world: a still mostly unrealized space (perhaps largely electronic) where national borders prove far less definitive than in our age of checkpoints and steel barriers. Wandering might provide a metaphoric language appropriate to this new digital and post-digital future, like untraceable cyber currencies or evanescent footsteps in a vagabond metaverse. Who can legitimately claim to be *essentially* French or English or American? Aren't we now, in our code-switching hybrid dialects and migratory waves, edging toward a digital citizenship where passports may seem like relics of an archaic system of nation-states?

Wanderers in such a transnational future—assuming it avoids nuclear implosion or asphyxiation by greenhouse gases—may celebrate the Romani people as demonstrating how to live well and passionately beneath the radar and off the grid, mobile and widely dispersed but unified in soul and culture, surviving by improvisation despite legal oppression, local prejudice, and vigilante terror—all of which, as it begins to appear, they have learned how to outlast and to surmount.

Notes

1 See Becky Taylor, Another Darkness, Another Dawn: A History of Gypsies, Roma and Travellers (London: Reaktion Books, 2014); and Isabel Fonseca, Bury Me Standing: The Gypsies and Their Journey (New York: Alfred A. Knopf, 1995).
2 Fonseca, Bury Me Standing, 5.
3 Clay Boland (lyrics) and Moe Jaffe (music), "Gypsy in My Soul" (1937), https://www.lyrics.com/lyric/2376939/Ella+Fitzgerald/Gypsy+in+My+Soul.
4 See Dick Sullivan, "Matthew Arnold, 'The Scholar Gipsy,' and the Cumnor Hills," *Victorian Web*, 11 August 2008, https://victorianweb.org/authors/arnold/sullivan2.
5 Matthew Arnold, "The Scholar-Gipsy," in The Poems of Matthew Arnold, ed. Kenneth and Miriam Allott, 2nd edn (London: Longman, 1979), ll.171–180.
6 Andrew Carnegie, Autobiography of Andrew Carnegie (Cambridge: Houghton Mifflin, 1920), 299.
7 Roger Miller, "King of the Road" (1965), https://genius.com/Roger-miller-king-of-the-road-lyrics.

17 Lines, circles, and boxes

Wandering seems to possess its own particular geometry that differs from the geometry of more settled states. Whether they are psychogeographers drifting along Paris streets or nomads moving across a desert landscape, wanderers tend to share a trait so obvious that it often goes unnoticed: an aversion to a geometry dominated by straight lines and right angles. A geometry of wandering strongly prefers serpentine, flowing lines, with corners smoothed into sinuous curves.

It is difficult—not impossible but difficult—to wander without deviating from a straight and narrow path. Digression, or *stepping away*, is almost as necessary to wandering as occasional direct routes to wander away from. The open road differs in its irregular geometries (accommodating the uneven flow of the terrain) from a superhighway, with its engineered straightaways. A geometry of wandering need not reflect or perpetuate traditional biases, as when we describe dishonesty as *crooked* and honesty as *straight and narrow*. Wandering no doubt reinforces its transgressive reputation by almost inescapable deviations. Wanderers, both as individuals and as groups, seem to possess a strong preference for whatever is curved, sinuous, off the beaten path or, especially, circular.

Native Americans once inhabited a geometry of sacred circles. Although the Ancestral Puebloan builders at Chaco Canyon in New Mexico constructed multistoried stone structures with rectangular walls, they reserved the circular form for the sacred belowground kivas. It was not an arbitrary choice. "Everything the Power of the World does is done in a circle," says the elderly Lakota Sioux holy man Black Elk, in a series of interviews published in 1932:

> The sky is round, and I have heard that the earth is round like a ball, and so are all the stars. The wind, in its greatest power, whirls. Birds make their nests in circles, for theirs is the same

DOI: 10.4324/9781003255307-17

> religion as ours. The sun comes forth and goes down again in a circle. The moon does the same, and both are round. Even the seasons form a great circle in their changing, and always come back again to where they were.

The geometry of circles implies both a theology and a cosmology well suited to a nomadic lifestyle.

The traditional circular vision of Native Americans is hardly unique to indigenous people. Ralph Waldo Emerson, educated at the Boston Public Latin School, at Harvard College, and at Harvard Divinity School, could rival Black Elk in his praise of circular forms. "The eye is the first circle," he writes, "the horizon which it forms is the second; and throughout nature this primary figure is repeated without end. It is the highest emblem in the cipher of the world."[1] *Cipher* is an Arabic word meaning "zero," and it comes to denote a code or secret system of encryption, much like the zeroes in binary computer codes. Ciphers or zeros are little circles that unlock bigger circles: secrets or even cosmic, transcendental mysteries. The world, for Emerson, is a cipher, in the sense that its material geometry of curvatures unlocks the immaterial world of spirit. Keys, a sign of sedentary lifestyles and construction, embody a metallic geometry of straight lines and indented rectangles engineered to open only a single, prefabricated, mechanical lock.

Black Elk, raised in the open spaces of Nebraska, simply assumes that humans and their impermanent, moveable dwellings will respect the circular patterns of the earth from which they are inseparable. "The life of a man is a circle from childhood to childhood," he explains:

> and so it is in everything where power moves. Our tepees were round like the nests of birds, and these were always set in a circle, the nation's hoop, a nest of many nests, where the Great Spirit meant for us to hatch our children.

These circular patterns, common and traditional among many Native American tribes, carry a significance as self-evident in their spiritual geometries as the soaring perpendiculars of medieval Gothic cathedrals.

Black Elk lives to see the circle shattered. A relentless western movement of white settlers—along with deliberately genocidal US policies and military campaigns—kill many thousands of indigenous people and drive the survivors onto bleak reservations. As a survivor of the 1890 Wounded Knee massacre, when US Army troops killed 250 Lakota Sioux men, women, and children, Black Elk understood the wider trajectory of loss by the superior weapons and the cunning betrayals of the *wasichus*, as he calls whites. He knows that the sacred circle is irrevocably broken as he watches his people herded into government housing units. "Wasichus," he says, "have put us in these square boxes. Our power is gone and we are dying, for the power is not in us any more."[2]

Square boxes. Anglo-European cultures so regularly build structures employing a square or rectangular design that our passion for right angles passes almost without notice. Black Elk notices, and he interprets the rectangle as a kind of *wasichu* prison or jail. The upright prison bar—like a ribbed metal fence—is almost an archetype of a western geometry designed to prevent fugitives from escaping or, in effect, just wandering off. Walls often serve as upright structures built by upright people to stop or jail "crooks" and wanderers who deviate from the straight and narrow.

An engineering logic underlies the architecture of circles and squares. Circles work best for one-room, single-space plans, just as right angles work best for multiroom and multilevel structures. In both the Eastern and Western worlds, early temples, chapels, and smaller shrines often employ a circular design. Tepees, igloos, and yurts similarly employ one-room, single-space, circular designs, which provide stability while also permitting quick construction and fast, easy relocation. Speed matters to nomadic people who often need to move abruptly. Tent-like structures, of course, need not be circular, but even rectangular tents are often designed for mobility and for ease of movement.

Rectangular structures, by contrast, are usually built of rigid materials—brick, stone, wood, or adobe—permitting the creation of quasi-permanent multiroom, multilevel structures. Medieval cathedrals not only soar upwards but also convey a sense of permanence, like stone simulacra of immobility. They assign to the sacred a limited site, *in perpetuum*. On a secular level, multilevel buildings regularly serve as storage facilities, allowing sedentary cultures (like the Pueblo people of the American Southwest) to heap up provisions for later distribution. The oldest surviving structures in northwestern Europe are two early Neolithic rectangular stone buildings in Scotland known as Knap of Howar: a farmhouse and an adjacent storage unit. Their straight sides perfectly answer the needs of people who plan to raise crops, to shelter herds, and to stay put. The two stone structures have stayed put for over 5,000 years.

"Indeed the straight line has emerged as a virtual icon of modernity, an index of the triumph of rational, purposeful design over the vicissitudes of the natural world."[3] Tim Ingold, an anthropologist, is surely correct about the iconic status of straight lines as a testament to the modern world and its vertical skyscrapers. In defense of circles, Black Elk might point to the tepee and the kiva as also iconic structures—employing a rational, purposeful design, respecting the natural world, and harboring no need or intent to achieve triumph.

The hard issue, beneath the shifting geometries of curved and straight, is land. Land is the inescapable bedrock of human habitation, sedentary or nomadic, and the hard issue is how we live *in relation to* the land. The questions do not concern where we live or in what kind of structure, but rather—as Heidegger writes in a challenging, difficult essay written long before the invention of deep ecology—how *to dwell.*[4]

Dwelling (as an action or state of being) differs significantly from owning a house or simply living in house-like structures, which we often describe as dwellings. Ownership is a legal or economic relationship that implies rights of possession. Dwelling, by contrast, makes no legal claims of possession, and its implications extend beyond a material construction to a basic relationship between humans and the land. (The land, for Heidegger, includes sky, spirit, and the built environment.) We *dwell*—whether in a skyscraper, in a tepee, or in a homeless shelter—as a larger expression of what Heidegger sees as a conscious relation to the land. Land, in this sense, is not a commodity to own or even a rented place to call our own. It is, in the ideal relationship that Heidegger invokes, a site for dwelling.

Wandering introduces a third term—beyond possessing and dwelling—to describe a possible human relation to the land. A utopian assurance implicit in possessing finds expression, literally, in the concept of a Promised Land. The Promised Land is frequently adopted as a metaphor to express the longing for a spiritual homeland, whether in heaven or in a future egalitarian social order, but its origins in the biblical exodus from Egypt raise serious questions no matter how the metaphor is applied. It is easy to forget or ignore that God requires (as a precondition of His promise) that the Israelites, upon arrival in the Promised Land, must drive out the current occupants:

> Then ye shall drive out all the inhabitants of the land from before you, and destroy all their pictures, and destroy all their molten images, and quite pluck down all their high places:
>
> And ye shall dispossess the inhabitants of the land, and dwell therein: for I have given you the land to possess it.[5]

Yahweh backs up this divine order (delivered directly to Moses) with threats. Even a utopian longing for freedom and justice, however, needs to ask whether arrival in the so-called promised land will require driving out the current occupants—especially if they do not share your ideas of justice and freedom. A wanderer, frankly, doesn't care which faith claims a disputed hill—which, of course, helps explain why wanderers are generally scorned by all settled parties. The question, from a wanderer's point of view, is why apparently the only viable human relation to land is to own it, sell it, occupy it, or possess it. Who gets to decide which people will be driven off the land and to whom it was once, apparently, promised?

Wandering, in its outsider status, has questions for nomadic people or tribes, such as Black Elk and the Lakota Sioux, who tend to regard certain broad territories as a homeland. Ancestors of the Lakota Sioux likely migrated from the lower Mississippi toward the Great Lakes and then northward again into the Dakotas. Starting around 1730, when the Cheyenne introduced them to horses, the Lakota lived in close relation to buffalo herds. Their traditional sacred and circular lifeways, as reflected in the words of Black Elk, may well offer a paradigm of wise dwelling, but if so, it was an unstable paradigm, incapable of withstanding the threats posed by a fast-moving settler culture whose relation to the land was to possess and to occupy it. The question for a wanderer is how far it is possible to dwell on the land, wisely or unwisely, if the land is swept away beneath your feet.

Anthropologist Keith Basso has shown how the landscape of Western Apache people in the American Southwest is mapped not with named roads or survey stakes but with stories: stories that most often convey the moral wisdom of an oral culture that teaches conduct indirectly, through narratives.[6] The settlers who claimed to own both the boxes they lived in and the land beneath the boxes told stories too. Different stories. Their stories eventually even allowed them to buy and sell "rights" to the air above the very tall boxes they erected in Manhattan.[7] "The land was ours before we were the land's," as poet Robert Frost puts it in "The Gift Outright" (1923). It is the poem he read in his eighties at the 1961 presidential inauguration of John F. Kennedy, when the bright sunlight dazzled his eyes and he lost his place, disoriented.

The land was *ours*? A new promised land? Exactly who, the wanderer might ask, promised it? To whom? Who dwelt on the land before settlers arrived to take possession of what was theirs before the land, apparently, possessed them? The wanderer does not so much dwell *on* the land as move *over* or *across* it. Unlike both the farmer and the rancher, locked in their endless struggle for possession, the wanderer drifts along like an ordinary cowpoke or even like a fancy singing cowboy—with the tumbling tumbleweeds.

Notes

1 "Circles" (1841), in Essays by Ralph Waldo Emerson, Introduction by Irwin Edman (1926; rpt. New York: Harper Perennial, 1951), 212. This single volume contains both the First Series (1841) and Second Series (1844).
2 John G. Neihardt, Black Elk Speaks: The Complete Edition (Lincoln: University of Nebraska Press, 2014), 121–122. Black Elk Speaks was first published in 1932. For questions of how far Neihardt altered Black Elk's words or thoughts, see The Sixth Grandfather: Black Elk's Teachings Given to John G. Neihardt, ed. Raymond J. DeMallie (Lincoln: University of Nebraska Press, 1984).
3 Tim Ingold, Lines: A Brief History (New York: Routledge, 2007), 152.
4 Martin Heidegger, "Building Dwelling Thinking" (1954), in Poetry, Language, Thought, trans. Albert Hofstadter (New York: Harper & Row, 1971), 143–162.
5 Numbers 33:52–53. This quotation is from the King James Version (1611).
6 Keith H. Basso, Wisdom Sits in Places: Landscape and Language Among the Western Apache (Albuquerque: University of New Mexico Press, 1996).
7 Theodore Steinberg, Slide Mountain, or, the Folly of Owning Nature (Berkeley: University of California Press, 1995), 135–165.

18 Wordsworth's wanderers

"I too have been a wanderer…."[1] So writes William Wordsworth, then in his early 30s, in the 1802 version of his autobiographical epic, The Prelude. Wandering did not diminish his poetic output, which fills a standard paperback volume over two inches thick. His ambitions extended further. As the crowning achievement of a writerly life that lasted into his seventies, he proposed a vast three-part magnum opus entitled The Recluse. This "philosophical poem," as he calls it, would take as its main subject "the sensations and opinions of a poet living in retirement"—no doubt a poet with more than a passing resemblance to the elderly William Wordsworth in his Lake District cottage.

It is no surprise that Wordsworth—a great poet but lacking superpowers—never finished The Recluse. He did finish part two: a nine-book narrative poem that he published separately in 1814, titled The Excursion. It is not among his more beloved works. Francis Jeffrey, editor of the *Edinburgh Review* from 1803 to 1829 and no friend to Romantic poets, dispatched The Excursion in a review that includes what scholar Jonathan Bate calls among "the most devastating opening sentences" ever written. Jeffrey needs only five crisp syllables to eviscerate The Excursion: "This will never do."[2]

The main character in The Excursion is an itinerant rural pedlar known only as the Wanderer. Now retired after a lifetime on the road, he remains vigorous and healthy in his seventies, "for travel unimpaired."[3] His health and travel-readiness are not mere incidental facts. The Wanderer has received his shaping education in nature, born in the Scottish highlands and (starting at age six) spending each summer in the mountains. "What wonder," as the narrator drives home the key Wordsworthian lesson about the educational powers of nature, "if his being thus became/ Sublime and comprehensive!" (I.233–234). It is exactly the same wandering education, although by lakes and sandy shores, that Coleridge wished for his infant son Hartley in "Frost at Midnight."

DOI: 10.4324/9781003255307-18

Nature constitutes only half of the Wordsworthian curriculum. The Wanderer, as an itinerant pedlar, augments his education in nature by conversing daily with local villagers, who (presumably) embody manners and minds free from urban, industrial corruptions. A dual formation in nature and society, as his trade takes him far and wide, makes the pedlar sound a bit like a modern rural Odysseus: "From his native hills/ He wandered far; much did he see of men,/ Their manners, their enjoyments, and pursuits,/ Their passions and their feelings; chiefly those/ Essential and eternal in the heart…" (I.340–344).

Wordsworth in the 1802 "Preface" to Lyrical Ballads argued for a new poetry free from previous traditions of poetic diction and employing a "language really spoken by men." The Wanderer, through an education in nature supplemented by far-reaching engagement with uncorrupted villagers, has the endowments of an ideal poet without the pesky interference of citified reviewers such as Francis Jeffrey, born in Edinburgh, educated at the University of Glasgow and Queen's College (Oxford), an attorney by profession and a failed London journalist before landing at the *Edinburgh Review*. Wandering, however, while crucial to the education of the Wanderer, cuts two ways in The Excursion. It places the Wanderer within Wordsworth's gallery of semi-heroic local sages, but it introduces a contrasting figure for whom wandering is both unheroic and a sign of rural lives gone disastrously awry. Her name is Margaret.

Margaret, whose story the Wanderer recounts at length, constitutes almost an Anti-Wanderer. She is introduced as a woman of "steady mind,/ Tender and deep in her excess of love" (I.513–514), who lives with her husband and child in a rural cottage, where they are tenant farmers. The Wanderer enjoys stopping on his travels to visit Margaret and her frugal, industrious family. Two seasons of blighted crops followed by war—calamities far beyond their control—soon, however, plunge the family into poverty. When a second child arrives, the husband falls ill and, half-crazed, is left to "wander here and there among the fields" (I.584). He finally abandons his family and enlists in a troop of soldiers. Margaret briefly considers following him—to share "the misery of that wandering life" (I.681)—and even considers suicide. Destitute, she too is transformed by suffering.

"I've wandered much of late" (I.754), Margaret explains to the Wanderer as he stops at the cottage after hearing the cry of an ailing child whom Margaret has left untended. She admits her thoughts of suicide, which only her "best prayers" (I.756) manage to fend off. Wordsworth does not sugarcoat the hardships of a rural life, vulnerable to weather, crop failures, rent collectors, and war. Margaret's wanderings, moreover, fail to provide the sustenance that travel provides for the Wanderer. Soon she has nothing left: "I have been travelling far; and many days/ About the fields I wander, knowing this/ Only, that what I seek I cannot find;/ And so I waste my time..." (I.764–767). Wandering for Margaret means insolation, waste, fear, and catastrophe.

The Excursion dramatizes two modes of wandering. The Wanderer embodies the positive model—sustaining in its contact with nature and the human heart. Margaret embodies the negative model—wandering as all but lethal in its potential isolation and anxieties. Even love in its domestic versions fails her, as Margaret spends her days hoping vainly for the return of her lost husband. Her sick child dies. She lives on alone for some nine years more, spinning hemp for a pittance as the once happy cottage decays around her. As the narrator puts it mildly: "Needs must it have been/ A sore heart-wasting!" (I.874–875).

Wandering in its harmful, distracted, destructive mode, such as depicted in Margaret's tale, is not an idiosyncratic Wordsworthian concern but reflects a larger Romantic interest in isolated wanderers, possibly even distant or close relations of Cain. Brahms's *Alto Rhapsody* (1869)—based upon a poem by Goethe—captures the self-destructive possibilities of wandering in a composition that follows the story of a solitary young misanthropic wanderer. The first two sections, sometimes described as chromatically dense and wandering, proceed for solo voice and orchestra in a C-minor key. In the third and final section, however, Brahms provides a resolution that Wordsworth denies to Margaret. The wanderer returns to the social world, and his return is marked by the entry of an all-male chorus, as the C-minor key resolves into a rich, melodious C major. Margaret, denied a C-major key, does not survive her extended wandering trauma.

Romantic wandering places the wanderer within another potentially lethal dilemma. It can prove as harmful to stop wandering as to wander. "O what can ail thee, knight-at-arms,/ Alone and palely loitering?" So asks the narrator in Keats's "La Belle Dame sans Merci" (1819), where loitering is the opposite or antithesis of the wandering life of a traditional knight errant. Eros in its bittersweet mode has frozen the knight in a fatal attraction. Nature in his case provides no solace but only a mirror of his desolate immobility: "The sedge has withered from the lake,/ And no birds sing."[4] Stasis, like wandering for Margaret, brings its own strange variety of suffering.

Suffering is the dilemma that brings out Wordsworth's most powerful writing in The Excursion. The poem contains one exceptionally strange moment when Wordsworth's narrator, in reflecting on the Wanderer's concern for Margaret, says that he "could *afford* to suffer/

With those whom he saw suffer" (I.370–371). The word *afford* is jarring. What does it mean to say, almost in economic terms, one can *afford* to share another person's suffering? The larger question might be posed in different terms. Is there a cost to the person who witnesses unrelieved suffering? The almost automatic response from ethicists today is to assert that we face almost a moral obligation to feel and express empathy. Wordsworth takes a different approach. Empathy will do nothing to restore Margaret's sanity or reassemble her disintegrated family: both are utterly lost. Empathy also may do nothing to console her in the insane grip of utter loss. The empathy that may be useless to the sufferer meanwhile may exact an enormous emotional toll on the witness who helplessly watches another person's suffering. Suffering is a question too serious to address with the catch-all obligation of empathy.

The jarring word *afford*—"he could *afford* to suffer/ With those whom he saw suffer"—suggests that what steadies the pedlar as he witnesses Margaret's suffering is his dual natural and social education as a wanderer. His wandering in effect supplies what anthropologists call an *affordance*: a supplemental use. A chair, for example, can supply a supplemental use or affordance as a step stool. The Wanderer's crucial dual education, in this sense, supplies a crucial affordance that allows him, as a witness, to experience an empathetic response to suffering that otherwise might utterly deplete or undo him.

This darker Wordsworth, aware of the emotional toll that suffering entails for the witness, takes readers into a poetic territory beyond the delight inspired by a chance encounter with ten thousand dancing daffodils. Margaret, by no fault of her own, happens into a life in which she is alone, abandoned by her husband, caring for two children, impoverished, nearly demented, close to suicidal, and undefended against a sorrow for which there is no earthly relief and which ultimately destroys her. The Wanderer is at least able to afford the emotional costs of his role as a compassionate witness, which is no small gift of a wandering life.

Francis Jeffrey is probably correct in his overall judgment about The Excursion. Wordsworth is beloved by many readers as a poet of consolation, however, and it is important to recognize that consolation for Wordsworth implies more than an open heart. The heart must be prepared in advance, with resources that supply an affordance when the costs of compassion come due. It might seem extravagant when Wordsworth in "Tintern Abbey" praises nature as the almost anthropomorphic "nurse," "guide," and "guardian" of his heart, his soul, and all his "moral being."[5] But the Wanderer's capacity to supply a compassionate witness to Margaret's terrible fate suggests how nature can indeed serve as nurse, guide, and guardian of the moral feelings. Wandering in The Excursion is not an activity that implies a self-justifying Whitmanesque democratic freedom and self-mastery. Wandering, as it informs the heart, offers a form of learning—an education really—developing the resources that, if we do not turn away from suffering in a soul-crushing neglect, can allow us to be present in the face of another person's unrelievable suffering. No small gift.

Notes

1 William Wordsworth, The Prelude: The Four Texts (1798, 1799, 1805, 1850), ed. Jonathan Wordsworth (London: Penguin, 1995), VI.261. The quotation here follows the 1802 text and remains unchanged (except for punctuation) in 1850.
2 Quoted in Jonathan Bate, Radical Wordsworth: The Poet Who Changed the World (New Haven, CT: Yale University Press, 2020), 376.
3 Wordsworth, "The Excursion" (1814), in The Collected Poems of William Wordsworth (Ware, Hertfordshire: Wordsworth Editions Limited, 1994), I.34. Further quotations are documented within the text.
4 John Keats, "La Belle Dame sans Merci" (1819), in The Complete Poems, ed. John Barnard, 3rd edn (New York: Penguin Books, 1988), ll.1–4.
5 Wordsworth, "Lines Composed a Few Miles above Tintern Abbey, On Revisiting the Banks of the Wye during a Tour, July 13, 1798," in The Collected Poems of William Wordsworth, ll.109–111.

19 The fallen

Wandering maintains an inseparable (if often inactive) relationship with falling. The drifting state of consciousness that welcomes happenstance and the accidental—say, stumbling upon a host of golden daffodils—also provides an opening for *bad* accidents. Accidents are a regular and unwelcome feature of the road. Even with a subliminal gaze, walkers recognize uneven pavement and zigzag to avoid sidewalk mishaps: in effect, they predict accidents and take steps *not to fall.* Falls, however, are probable events that accompany wandering no matter what the precautions, since wandering so often makes forays into unfamiliar territories. Mere stumbles can initiate unanticipated, precipitous descents into calamity. Three loud knocks on your illegally parked van likely means a visit from the police. The road is not a smooth straightaway but, on occasion, an asphalt mirage suspended over a deathtrap. Wanderers can't avoid falling. They are often listed among the fallen, just as the fallen often take to the road as wanderers.

"First came the man: a young wanderer in a fatigue coat and long hair. Then came the legend, as John Rambo sprang from the pages of First Blood to take his place in the American cultural landscape." It is dust jacket prose—not entirely accurate, but a fair introduction to the franchise-launching character John Rambo. Rambo makes his initial appearance in David Morrell's 1972 novel, and ten years later he appears on screen in *First Blood*, starring Sylvester Stallone, which, in turn, initiates a cinema bonanza that concludes—almost 50 years after Morrell's novel—with *Rambo: Last Blood* (2019), if it truly *is* the last. Canadian-born Morrell did not serve in Vietnam, but some of his students at the University of Iowa did, and the systematic mayhem that accompanies Rambo has its origins in the Vietnam War. "The man who trained him kills him in the end," Morrell says discussing Rambo's death in the novel, which the filmmakers of course ignored: "The whole point is that the system who created Rambo destroys him."[1]

DOI: 10.4324/9781003255307-19

Rambo as the novel opens is less a classic Romantic wanderer than a homeless drifter. Hostile and jobless after his military discharge, he goads the local sheriff into charging him with vagrancy. Police custody goes badly: he slices open a deputy's stomach, and his hasty escape initiates the extended chase sequence that drives the novel. A wandering vagrant becomes a fugitive on the run. "One morning he found he had wandered in a circle," Morrell writes, "and after that he travelled only in the day."[2] Fugitives wander, ever since Cain, but wandering in circles (with the law hot on your trail) is not a smart tactic in a bloody chase narrative that replays hard-nosed sheriffs tracking a quasi-sympathetic but doomed outlaw. The filmmakers help by supplying Rambo with acceptable victims—not (as in the novel) police officers and national guard troops.

War—cut loose from chase narratives—regularly creates wanderers. Rambo as a Vietnam vet has experienced both wartime trauma and the prior military training that help create the hostile, self-divided drifter whom a hostile, self-divided nation abandons on his return home. Readers tempted to recognize in Rambo the signs of posttraumatic stress disorder (PTSD) might consider that PTSD is officially recognized as a mental health condition only in 1980, five years after the Vietnam War ends.[3] The US Department of Veterans Affairs reports that 15% of Vietnam veterans will suffer from PTSD, and the Vietnam War alone has produced 47% of the current homeless veterans in America.[4] The larger point: all wars create veterans whose wounds extend both inward and outward, and one outward sign of military trauma is homelessness. Shell shock entered the medical lexicon with World War I, while World War II generated new quasi-medical terms such as combat fatigue and war neurosis.[5] No doubt the American Civil War generated similar psychic damage in a conflict that kills 2% of the population, as an entire nation adjusts to the uncanny pageant of traumatized, jobless, homeless wanderers.

War transforms soldiers into wanderers. Facts and figures change, but the principle remains stable. The US military, good at keeping track, reports that in 2009, on any given night, some 131,000 veterans were homeless.[6] The shocking number has been going down, keeping pace with a general downward national trend in homelessness.[7] In January 2019, on any given night, some 37,085 veterans were homeless, with (another turn of the screw) nine out of ten homeless vets male and one-third African American.[8] Today, in the US over 30% of the homeless men camping in doorways or sleeping on sidewalks are veterans. Most are single and poor, and almost half suffer from mental illness or from substance abuse. Wars are machines for the production of wanderers.[9] The system that killed John Rambo also produced him, just as David Morrell says.

War is not the only social machine for producing homelessness. Housing is a fundamental human right, according to the European Parliament, but figures released in 2020 indicate that every night in Europe more than 700,000 people are "sleeping rough" (as it's called): an increase of 70% over the last ten years.[10] Sleeping is equally rough across the Atlantic. On any given night in 2020, some 580,000 people were homeless in the US—almost 40% on the street, in abandoned buildings, or otherwise unsheltered.[11] Nor are male veterans the only victims of wartime homelessness. Recurrent wars and conflict across Europe in the nineteenth century helped drive women (working traditional jobs as servants, factory laborers, and seamstresses) into the swelling ranks of streetwalkers.

"No work, no money, and no home."[12] So explained one female inmate confined for prostitution in New York's Blackwell's Island prison. Before entering the sex trade, one-quarter of the women in Dr. William Sanger's 1859 study of 2,000 prostitutes reported being "destitute."[13]

While destitute women wandered as economic casualties in a world basically run by men, the male-oriented social world created a special gendered category to contain apparently unruly or impoverished females: the fallen woman. From Paris and London to New York City as the dandified *flâneur* watched the crowded boulevards in detachment, an eerily familiar urban figure emerged whose social stigma now included both her affront to public morals and the danger she posed to public health. Verdi's *La traviata* (1853) reflects this gendered world in which "fallen"—far outside a theology of original sin—applies specifically to women. Verdi gives the "fallen" courtesan Violetta the upper hand in generosity of spirit, but of course she must die. In a new era that takes steps to protect "sex workers" and to medicalize "sex addiction," falling has become a more gender-inclusive category; Jessica Bruder found that elderly and downwardly mobile van-dwellers were often women. Today women constitute roughly 20% of the homeless population, with risk factors including alcohol abuse, drug abuse, and mental illness.[14] Women who are homeless also regularly fall prey to sexual exploitation. For homeless women, the road or street remains dangerous, especially for abused, neglected, and runaway teens.

Wandering and homelessness create equally dark futures for children. William Blake's chimney sweeper and Charles Dickens's Oliver Twist at least give childhood trauma a visible presence, but homelessness among children today has a malign invisibility. In the US, on any given night in January 2019, an estimated 53,692 family units (in the language of sociology) were homeless, many units including young children. Homeless children, even with an adult in the vicinity, often live in cars or in places otherwise not meant for human habitation.[15] No figures can count the street orphans, runaways, castaways, and sex-trafficked children who add an unquantifiable measure of misery and distress to the bare statistics. Children also number prominently among refugees surviving in tent cities and among migrant families fleeing poverty, drug gangs, and the devastation of climate change. Wandering children across the globe are not only voiceless—without political status or representation—but faceless: unseen, at least outside the designated UN offices and a few NGOs, as if the sight (minus a Wordsworthian affordance) is simply too unbearable.

Numbers can make us numb—the English words come from different roots—so it is encouraging that childhood homelessness is beginning to generate a modest body of writing for children. A Shelter in Our Car (2004) by Monica Gunning describes Zettie, a young girl who (after her father's death) leaves Jamaica with her mother for New York City. There, she lives with her mother in their car. In The Red Pencil (2014) Andrea Davis Pinkney tells the versified story of 12-year-old Amira, who lives with her family in a rural village in Sudan amid unseen but easily identified dangers:

> My mother says,
> "The Janjaweed attack without warning.
> If ever they come—run."[16]

The Janjaweed attack, burn the village, kill the livestock, and start Amira on a dangerous journey to a refugee camp. It is a story of eventual recovery, like the tale of Zettie, since children's literature in the post-Grimm era generally steers clear of violent, unhappy endings. Adults writing for and about children regularly endorse such a perspective, as if children must be raised on fantasies and half-truths. ("The Janjaweed are bad people, Muma says" [58].) It's an ancient conflict—simmering ever since farmer Cain killed nomadic herder Abel. The Janjaweed are nomads, and Amira's family raises crops. Some children today have limited access to new visual forms of self-expression and self-representation, hardly unmediated, but how many refugee children will share Amira's good fortune? How many girls like Zettie will ever find a stable home?

Wandering among children is not confined to refugees, but even the number of refugee children worldwide is staggering. 17 million children were among the international refugees and asylum seekers in 2019. Another 16 million children live among international migrants.[17] Nearly 50 million children worldwide, according to UNICEF figures for 2016, have migrated across borders or been forcibly displaced—a conservative estimate.[18] One hundred million children worldwide live on the streets, according to a 1989 estimate. The figure, as the Consortium for Street Children advises, is considerably outdated: "The true numbers are unknown."[19]

"There was a child went forth every day," writes Walt Whitman in Leaves of Grass (1855), "And the first object he looked upon and received with wonder or pity or love or dread, that object he became…."[20] Whitman wrote this passage seized with optimism, almost a decade before he volunteered to care for maimed and dying soldiers during the Civil War. What do homeless and wandering children across the globe see as they go forth every day to become what they see? The phrase *poster child* was unknown before 1938, and images of distressed children no doubt help today in fundraising. Images designed to tug at the heartstrings of donors have their place, but the situation is dire. Children are prominent among the fallen. Their wandering is not a personal choice but a result of adult failures. The adult world needs to pause its endless wars to address—urgently, effectively, and head-on—the crisis of homeless children that it has created. Wandering has no worse worst-case scenario than a child left to wander alone and homeless.

Notes

1 Niall Browne, "FIRST BLOOD Author David Morrell Talks RAMBO – Part 1," *Movies in Focus*, 14 November 2018, https:// www.moviesinfocus.com/interview-first-blood-author-david-morrell-talks-rambo-part-1/.
2 David Morrell, First Blood (1972; rpt. New York: Grand Central Publishing, 2017), 47.
3 US Department of Veterans Affairs, "PTSD and Vietnam Veterans: A Lasting Issue 40 Years Later," https://www.publichealth.va.gov/exposures/publications/agent-orange/agent-orange-summer-2015/nvvls.asp.
4 US Department of Veterans Affairs, "How Common Is PTSD in Veterans?," https://www.ptsd.va.gov/understand/common/common_veterans.asp.
5 Erin Blakemore, "How PTSD Went from 'Shell-Shock' to a Recognized Medical Diagnosis," *National Geographic*, 16 June 2020, https://www.nationalgeographic.com/history/article/ptsd-shell-shock-to-recognized-medical-diagnosis.
6 National Coalition for the Homeless, "Homeless Veterans," September 2009, https://www.nationalhomeless.org/factsheets/veterans.pdf.
7 National Alliance to End Homelessness, "State of Homelessness: 2020 Edition," https://endhomelessness.org/homelessness-in-america/homelessness-statistics/state-of-homelessness-2020/.

8 US Department of Housing and Urban Development, The 2019 Annual Homeless Assessment Report (AHAR) to Congress, January 2020, https://www.huduser.gov/portal/sites/default/files/pdf/2019-AHAR-Part-1.pdf.

9 See National Coalition for the Homeless, "Homeless Veterans" (previously cited).

10 European Parliament, "How Parliament Wants to End Homelessness in the EU," 24 November 2020, https://www.europarl.europa.eu/news/en/headlines/society/20201119STO92006/how-parliament-wants-to-end-homelessness-in-the-eu.

11 US Department of Housing and Urban Development, The 2020 Annual Homeless Assessment Report (AHAR) to Congress, January 2021, https://www.huduser.gov/portal/sites/default/files/pdf/2020-AHAR-Part-1.pdf.

12 Anya Jabour, "Women's Work and Sex Work in Nineteenth-Century America," *Mercy Street Revealed,* 22 February 2016, https://www.pbs.org/mercy-street/blogs/mercy-street-revealed/womens-work-and-sex-work-in-nineteenth-century-america.

13 See, among other texts, Judith R. Walkowitz, Prostitution and Victorian Society: Women, Class, and the State (New York: Cambridge University Press, 1980); and Meredith Dank, Jennifer Yahner, Kuniko Madden, Isela Bañuelos, Lilly Yu, Andrea Ritchie, Mitchyll Mora, and Brendan Conner, Surviving the Streets of New York: Experiences of LGBTQ Youth, YMSM, YWSW Engaged in Survival Sex (New York: Urban Institute, 2015).

14 Carol L. M. Caton, Patrick E. Shrout, Boanerges Dominguez, Paula F. Eagle, Lewis A. Opler, and Francine Cournos, "Risk Factors for Homelessness Among Women with Schizophrenia," *American Journal of Public Health* 85, no. 8 (1995): 1153–1156.

15 National Alliance to End Homelessness, "Children and Families," https://endhomelessness.org/homelessness-in-america/who-experiences-homelessness/children-and-families/.

16 Andrea Davis Pinkney, The Red Pencil (New York: Little, Brown and Company, 2014), 61.

17 UNICEF, "Child Migration," April 2020, https://data.unicef.org/topic/child-migration-and-displacement/migration/.

18 UNICEF, "Uprooted: The Growing Crisis for Refugee and Migrant Children," September 2016, https://data.unicef.org/resources/uprooted-growing-crisis-refugee-migrant-children/.

19 Consortium for Street Children, "About Street Children," https://www.streetchildren.org/about-street-children/.

20 Walt Whitman, "There Was a Child Went Forth," in Leaves of Grass, ed. David S. Reynolds (New York: Oxford University Press, 2005), 78.

20 Wandering while black

Wandering—if you are black in certain neighborhoods in the US—can get you killed. A race-based wandering rooted in the slave trade and its aftermath creates a situation in which the movement through space and place holds distinctively charged meanings for African Americans.

The Great Migration is a spontaneous mass movement between 1916 and 1970 in the US that brings six million blacks from the Jim Crow South to northern and western cities. Interior migrations are not unprecedented, although hardly similar. The Gold Rush from 1848 to 1855 saw some 300,000 people race to California. Under the Indian Removal Act (1830), the federal government moved some 16,000 Cherokee people to present-day Oklahoma from cotton-rich states east of the Mississippi River. The so-called Trail of Tears, which covered over 2,000 miles and nine states, claimed some 4,000 lives. It is now run by the National Park Service, with tourists advised to "plan your visit." There is no Park Service memorial to the millions of African Americans fleeing the racist South during the Great Migration.

The National Lynching Memorial, in Montgomery, Alabama, might stand as a shameful anti-memorial to the Great Migration. Between 1882 and 1968, white mobs mostly in the Deep South lynched 4,743 blacks. Murder and systematic terror at the hands of white Southerners are what drive six million blacks northward. As a white middle-class male raised in the northeast, I have no firsthand experience to help me understand this race-based, hate-driven migration. My limitations, however, reflect difficulties inherent in seeking to understand wandering as experienced by groups with distinctive histories of social intolerance (to put it mildly). The search takes you into unfamiliar places and unsettling experiences that thrust seekers into the ancient biblical role of sojourners in a strange land.

Slavery and the Great Migration, ironically, are experiences strange even to African Americans who now make their own intellectual and

DOI: 10.4324/9781003255307-20

emotional journeys of reverse migration to reclaim an understanding of their migrant or enslaved ancestors.

Wandering is probably not the right term to describe the forced movement of African Americans, whether enslaved or the descendants of enslaved people, but it remains an image submerged not too far beneath the surface of multiple journeys still incomplete.

Morgan Jerkins and Saidiya Hartman are African American writers who undertake personal journeys to retrace ancestors transported in chains across the perilous Middle Passage or subsequently lost in the Great Migration. Their separate quests reflect larger difficulties in tracing the lives of enslaved and uprooted people whose histories disappear within the multiple erasures of the African American diaspora. Jerkins, born a generation after Hartman, in Wandering in Strange Lands (2020) travels in reverse (north to south) the journey that her ancestors took on the Great Migration, retracing their steps but also simultaneously seeking her own roots. She seeks, most of all, to uncover truths about her racial identity: "I have spent my career," she writes, "trying to tease out the interwoven threads of who I am as a black woman."[1]

Jerkins in her personal quest encounters continuous obstacles, which include incomplete records, unreliable memories, and even her own (troubling) fair skin, which together create unbridgeable gaps and dilemmas. Happily, she does encounter people who help fill in some of the missing information. Her title, however, recognizes that she faces (like her ancestors) the distinctive challenge of a social terrain in which black skin always places you in the role of stranger—even, in her case, partly a stranger to herself—making her a multiple or polymorphic wanderer.

Her immediate family ultimately wanders west to California, a secular promised land, while she doubly reverse migrates—not only north to south but also west to east—searching for the roots that never yield her a fully satisfying account and thus leave her, with her search impossible to complete, always in the position of a wanderer.[2]

"My family trail disappeared," writes Saidiya Hartman, "in the second decade of the nineteenth century."[3] She undertakes a journey across generations without recent threads of genealogy or even much family history as her guide. She is focused less on personal roots than on a broader understanding of slavery as a process of uprooting. Slavery, in her retelling, required as intrinsic to its operation a deliberate process of deracination. This strategy makes the entire current DNA-driven obsession with ancestry deeply frustrating for many blacks whose quests often hit dead ends. With no family connections earlier than the 1820s to guide her, Hartman reads deeply in documents about the slave trade and vividly portrays what enslavement meant for blacks. Her search, in the absence of a personal lineage, recovers a larger historical portrait of black experience. "The most universal definition of the slave," she writes, "is a stranger" (5).

Strangers, no matter how universal the role of wanderer, face distinctive historical and personal struggles. Hartman's stranger—"[t]orn from kin and community, exiled from one's country, dishonored and violated" (5)—is more than a generic outsider. The Fugitive Slave Act of 1850 defines escaped slaves as property. Runaway strangers legally defined as property—treated often like farm animals—fall into a special class of explicitly dehumanized wanderers. Frederick Douglass, even once safely escaped to a free state, lived at times like a fugitive, continually looking over his shoulder, poised to flee (as Douglass did) when southern slave catchers pressed too close. This is a distinctively African American fugitive wandering, predicated on slavery, with psychic consequences that extend across generations to as yet undiagnosed categories of posttraumatic stress disorder.

The impossibility of full freedom, even for freed blacks, is what Saidiya Hartman recognizes in her grandfather, who erased all contact with Africa, choosing to live in Curaçao as an itinerant seaman: "one place," as she imagines, "was as good as the next." She continues: "Maybe it was that he had no desire to put down roots or to reclaim them. He had embraced errancy or taking to the sea as the closest thing to freedom he would experience" (98). Errancy or wandering always entails an imperfect freedom, and Hartman's grandfather is doubly constrained by his black skin. Her own legacy of constraint is what Hartman seeks to overcome in a reverse migration never fully realized. She is startled to discover on first arriving in her ancestral homeland, Africa, that despite her black skin she too, as a foreigner, is now assigned to the shifting role of stranger.

Flashback to racially segregated Alabama during World War II. Herman Blount, a black man in his 20s, refuses the recently instituted military draft. The judge hearing his case says he should be drafted. Blount replies that he'd kill the first officer he meets:

> "I've never seen a nigger like you before," the judge said.
> "No," Blount replied, "and you never will again."[4]

Following the route of the Great Migration, Blount—a talented pianist—next appears as a jazz musician in Chicago, where in 1952 he adopts the name Sun Ra.

The name is far more than an exotic stage persona. Herman Blount disappears into a self-created identity with mythic black roots. Ra, the ancient Egyptian sun god, invokes not only a figure of cosmic power but also a transformative moment in his own personal journey. A bright beam, Sun Ra says, "a giant spotlight," suddenly turned his body transparent as space aliens transported him to Saturn. Otherworldly voices warned him that "complete chaos" was approaching. *Drop out of college*, the voices pressed, *and speak to the world through your music.* Sun Ra had no doubts about the message or the messengers: "They had one little antenna on each ear. A little antenna over each eye."

Sun Ra as a musician soon gained a reputation for his unusual range of mind. "His canon of must-reads," according to Ytasha L. Womack, "included books on theosophy, numerology, metaphysics, science fiction, biblical studies, and a glut of underground alternative history books and African history books."[5] He regularly conducted seminars for fellow musicians—some doubtless based on Martin Bernal's highly speculative three-volume Black Athena: The Afroasiatic Roots of Classical Civilization. (The first two volumes appeared in 1987 and 1991; Sun Ra did not live to read volume three, published in 2006.) Science fiction and its futuristic promise of new worlds also influenced both his music and his deliberately space-age appearance. Flashlights, solar helmets, star-shaped dark glasses, sparkling capes, and sci-fi gear helped express his foundational position in the movement that has come to be called Afrofuturism.[6]

Afrofuturists revere Sun Ra for his contribution in imagining a Second Great Migration. The historical northern migration that left blacks still profoundly unfree, in effect, offered the pattern for his vision of a subsequent and successful migration to a fully free future (Figure 20.1), described in often mysterious detail distributed within his extensive collected poetry and prose.[7]

Saturn and outer space held metaphoric power for Sun Ra as a poet and philosopher with no illusions about the position of blacks in the contemporary social world. "I'm not real," he tells skeptical blacks in the film that he cowrote, produced, and starred in, *Space Is the Place* (1974). He adds: "I'm just like you. You don't exist in this society."

Paradoxically, while his futuristic costumes make Sun Ra hard to ignore, the costumes also serve the strategic function of making black invisibility *visible.* He gives current black lives—unreal and nonexistent in a white-run world—an imagined new black future *elsewhere.* "I do not come to you as a reality," Sun Ra explains in *Space Is the Place.* "I come to you as the myth. Because that's what black

Figure 20.1 Sun Ra: Astro Black (1973, reissued 2018). Detail. Album Cover. Courtesy of Modern Harmonic. Photo: David Morris.

people are, myths." Metaphoric statements with overlapping multiple semantic layers belong to his stance as poet and prophet. In a partial translation: he claims that blacks are invisible today, and he too is invisible and thus unreal; he speaks as an unreal black man who nonetheless embodies the myth of a future black utopia in which all black people are fully realized and fully visible. Not surprisingly, he was not always well understood, which of course did not bother him.[8]

His flamboyant and outlandish figure on stage meanwhile constitutes the opening chapters in a new Afrofuturist narrative of black embodiment and power opposed to lives configured, today, in the contemporary social world as powerless, thin, and unreal. Sun Ra is hard *not* to see.

Myth fascinated Sun Ra as a medium for liberating truths, which helps account for his frequent references to William Blake.

Blake's "prophetic books" offer a cosmic myth—deeply puzzling to outsiders—that gestures toward an alternate future in which humans live as fully liberated beings. Blake too recognizes current social oppressions that deform the ideal human figure, and the medium of recognition, significantly, is figured as urban wandering: "I wander thro' each charter'd street,/ Near where the charter'd Thames does flow./ And mark in every face I meet/ Marks of weakness, marks of woe."[9] Sun Ra sees many similar woeful faces with his similarly wandering gaze. "You look out at the world," as he puts it, dropping into straight talk, "and you say, 'Something's wrong with this stuff.'" He is speaking in rehearsal to his jazz group, the Arkestra, and he adds, with implications that extend beyond music: "Then you get so mad you can play it on your instrument. Play some fire on it. If you're not mad at the world you don't have what it takes."[10]

The Thirteenth Amendment to the US Constitution, ratified 6 December 1865, marks the official abolition of slavery, but it did not abolish the organized murder of blacks, especially in the Deep South. White supremacist legislatures passed Jim Crow laws to oppress the mostly poor and illiterate new black citizens. Jobs were few, and African Americans voted with their feet. The first wave of migration (from 1916 to 1940) saw 1.6 million rural blacks move to New York, Detroit, Philadelphia, Chicago, Baltimore, and Cleveland. The second wave (from 1940 to 1970) saw another five million blacks migrate to northern cities as well as to several Mid-South cites such as Memphis and Louisville. South Carolina, North Carolina, and Georgia from 1940 to 1970 lost a major chunk of their black populations.

Sun Ra, beyond his musical reputation, is important for linking race and wandering with the mythic quest for a black utopia. The Great Migration, in effect, offers a founding metaphor that extends to the idealized future described in *Space Is the Place*: "a colony for black people."

Notes

1 Morgan Jerkins, Wandering in Strange Lands: A Daughter of the Great Migration Reclaims Her Roots (New York: HarperCollins, 2020), 134.
2 Jerkins, Wandering in Strange Lands, 209.
3 Saidiya Hartman, Lose Your Mother: A Journey Along the Atlantic Slave Route (New York: Farrar, Straus and Giroux, 2007), 7. Further quotations are documented within the text.
4 Quoted in Namwali Serpell, "Sun Ra: 'I'm Everything and Nothing,'" *New York Review of Books*, 23 July 2020.

5 Ytasha L. Womack, Afrofuturism: The World of Black Sci-Fi and Fantasy Culture (Chicago: Lawrence Hill Books, 2013), 59.

6 See Paul Youngquist, A Pure Solar World: Sun Ra and the Birth of Afrofuturism (Austin: University of Texas Press, 2016).

7 Sun Ra, The Immeasurable Equation: The Collected Poetry and Prose, ed. James L. Wolf and Hartmut Geerken (Norderstedt: Waitawhile, 2005).

8 "No figure before Ra had so thoroughly sanctified the concept of utopia and imagined it in a way that was virtually unrecognizable and unrealizable," writes Alex Zamalin. "And no one had defined it with such moral seriousness in ways that were so obscure and contradictory" (Black Utopia: The History of an Idea from Black Nationalism to Afrofuturism [New York: Columbia University Press, 2019], 96).

9 William Blake, "London" (1794), in The Complete Poetry and Prose of William Blake, ed. David V. Erdman, revised edn (Berkeley: University of California Press, 2008), ll.1–4.

10 Quoted in John F. Szwed, Space Is the Place: The Lives and Times of Sun Ra (New York: Pantheon Books, 1997), 100. For Sun Ra's trip to Saturn, see 29.

21 Accidental wanderers

Wanderers often don't plan on wandering. Wandering is eminently planless, which contributes to its appeal or terror, and sometimes it happens entirely by accident. Odysseus, an archetype of the wanderer, wanders for ten years after leaving Troy, all unplanned. The Homeric narrative describes him with the twin epithets *polymechanos* ("of many devices") and *polytropon* ("of many turns"), and he needs all his many turns and devices when he sets out for home and the accidents begin to rain down.

The Odyssey consists largely in the accidents and adventures that befall Odysseus on his wandering journey home. The accidents that beset him do not simply disrupt a return but rather threaten the completion of a significant ritual, since the *nostos* ("homecoming") holds a formal status in ancient Greek culture. Its failure or incompletion is as serious as an interrupted marriage ceremony. The circular arc of The Odyssey—basic to its "ring" composition—is suspended or broken until the homecoming completes it, unlike the linear, open-ended, zigzag pattern of a picaresque novel.[1] Wandering minus a homecoming leaves the hero resembling a bridegroom left at the altar: a ritual action is incomplete. The Odyssey concludes, in fact, not with the return but with the hero's reunion with his faithful wife, Penelope.

Accidental wanderers, as they do not choose to wander, differ from the wandering figure in Leaves of Grass who takes to the road as a self-selected exemplar of democratic freedom and self-mastery. Wandering is a condition that many wanderers more or less stumble into. It is possible, of course, to identify forces operating behind the scenes. Although wandering for Odysseus is a response to circumstances beyond his control, it is the gods who brew up the storms and direct the major accidents. Other wanderers might point to unseen forces directing their fate, from social class, capital markets, and psychic drives to the dead hand of the past. The crucial point: accidental wandering is potentially endless, even if wanderers seek an end to wandering.

DOI: 10.4324/9781003255307-21

Accidental wandering, in search of an ending, encodes a principle of entropy and seeks its own undoing. Ithaca as the longed-for destination represents numberless real or imagined harbors, shelters, asylums, or promised lands where wandering comes to a halt. Bobby McGee, who slips away from a hitchhiker's life, may or may not find the home he is looking for, but slipping away to find a home is at least not a temporary pause in a restless, open-ended life of accidental wandering. It is rather the crucial step toward a full stop. Wandering is often the search for an ending: arrival at a long-sought destination that, in effect, constitutes a way out.

Accidental wandering—unlike, say, a walking tour of London or a ramble through Central Park—may also coincide with an intellectual questioning. The questions can quickly escalate all the way to ontology—is *being* tied up with wandering?—but they can also focus on lesser issues of causation. Although Zeus orders the storm that blows Odysseus's 12 ships far off course as they leave Troy, it is Odysseus who orders an impromptu raid as he begins the homeward journey. After massacring the villagers, his warriors (drunk and sated) are easy prey to a nighttime counterattack by surviving villagers, who kill 72 Greeks. This deadly counterattack is what causes Odysseus to order a hasty escape to the open ocean: an unlucky decision, since Greek galleys (built for speed with low-slung hulls and flat keels) prove no match for the ensuing storm. Accidents and coincidences further tangle the threads of causation. Ever wily, concealing his true identity, Odysseus describes to King Alcinous the shipwreck that casts him, as sole survivor, on the isle of Calypso. "All of my comrades, my brave friends, were killed," he says.[2] This is a sanitized version. Odysseus has lost *all* of his 600 men. Are the gods or fate alone responsible for this dismal record as a commanding officer?

Questioning proliferates as philosophers take their turn in following the thread of accident and causation. "I don't know my way about": this is how Ludwig Wittgenstein describes the form that philosophical problems assume in his mind, which closely resembles wandering or getting lost.[3] Philosophers, at least since Nietzsche, are among the cultural figures designated to ponder big questions, and their common procedures—maybe in response to getting lost—include a process of philosophical wayfinding. Indeed, the act of questioning—*putting in question*—describes a standard procedure in modern philosophy. In this post-theological discourse, wandering for philosophers is often just what you do when you pose big questions, not knowing your way about, searching for a way out or way in, without a plan and proceeding more or less by accident. Wandering and subsequent wayfinding prove, for many modern thinkers, mutually entangled activities in which accidents not only cannot be excluded but also are valued for their contact with a realm of the open-ended and the unformulated.

"There are no facts," wrote Nietzsche, for whom openness and accident prove almost synonymous, "everything is in flux, incomprehensible, elusive...."[4] Wandering—not knowing your way about—defines the task of the philosopher after Nietzsche: less to pursue Truth with a capital T—Ultimate Closure—than to question human practices and values that seem resistant to thought, off-center, and in flux. Martin Heidegger, an admirer of Nietzsche, described an ideal course for philosophers this way: it is better for thinking not to establish itself in the beaten path of what appears true, understandable, or familiar, but rather "to wander into the strange...."[5]

Wandering into the strange—more or less a thumbnail description of what happens to Odysseus on his way home—implies dangers and discoveries inseparable from such excursions. The thinker for Heidegger (as scholar Gerald Bruns puts it) is "Cain-like, exposed, unhoused ... stumbling among fragments, skeptical, vulnerable (perhaps not just vulnerable) to madness, alien to serenity and comfort, abroad without ground, out of control...."[6] This is an unsettled state in which accidents come fast and thick. Minds open to unsettling questions, to random accidents, and to wandering into the strange can expect that discoveries will not likely resemble rational demonstrations (QED). They are likelier to resemble whatever (so to speak) falls out. The realm of the accidental—from Latin *accidere* (*ad* + *cadere,* "to fall")—embraces what we cannot control, cannot predict, and just, as it were, happens.

Accidental wandering, whether in thought or action, tends to require or produce a special form of solitude. Odysseus, in his solitary arrival home alone at Ithaca, attests to a crucial element of solitariness relevant to modern philosophers. The implicit mental rigors of wandering into the strange tend to isolate thinkers who, like Odysseus, must survive by their wits. There is not much company on Nietzsche's mountaintop. Jacques Derrida composed a tribute on the death of Gilles Deleuze—the inventor of nomad thought—describing the dilemma of various modern like-minded colleagues. Derrida always resisted efforts to identify him with the creation of a new code called deconstruction. The solitude and misunderstanding entailed in code-defying nomad thought suggests the value of a special kinship among nomadic thinkers: a remote fellowship of unaffiliated solitary wanderers. Derrida's tribute to Deleuze braids together a number of related threads, and its exact degree of irony remains incalculable.

The title of his tribute is fascinating nonetheless in its choice of metaphor: "I'm going to have to wander [*errer*] all alone."[7]

Derrida's infinitive *errer* embodies multiple resonances. *Errer* not only means "to wander" but also evokes an association—both in French and in English—with missteps and mistakes. *Errer* also has a close association in French with accident (*l'erreur*). The single word resembles a rich acoustic-semantic chord that unites *wandering* with *error* and *accident* in a single word, before Derrida closes the reverberation with the bare "all alone."

Philosophical wandering, while it cannot preclude error, sometimes finds a way—*within* the woods, not out of the woods—to clarities. Heidegger, who walked the wooded paths near his cabin in the Black Forest, described the encounter with truth as like a sudden *unconcealment*. Something hidden or forgotten suddenly reveals itself in startling clarity, as if a wanderer in the woods suddenly encountered a *clearing* (*die Lichtung*). So too truth or Being unconceals itself, Heidegger believed, as if Van Gogh's sketch of worn-out peasant shoes revealed, at a glance, the unconcealed truth about their owner. Such moments do not arrive like the conclusion to a chain of logical argument. Chains of logic are exactly what, after Nietzsche, philosophers seek to escape, often in elusive styles of writing that defy synopsis. Wandering thought leaves space open for what does not follow and what cannot be demonstrated.

Wandering is what Odysseus does: what just falls out. Minus the accidents and contingencies on his voyage home, however, he is little more than another Greek commander who sails to Troy and sails home again. His wandering is what creates the narrative. Wandering too is what modern philosophers do, even if they seek an intellectual point of rest or an elusive full stop. Still, there is no *nostos* or homecoming in modern philosophy, but mostly a commitment, as for Derrida, to keep on wandering, keep erring, and keep meeting the accidents where you find them (or where they find you).

An Odyssean archetype of accidental wandering in philosophy does not rule out modes of thinking that pay primary respect to design, reason, communication, and the grounds of knowledge, as in the work of Jürgen Habermas. Wandering remains the outlier, and thinking regularly aligns with the values of settlement. Accidental wandering or wandering in a realm of accidents does, however, identify a consistent strain in contemporary thought, especially among philosophers who—rather than focusing on logic or analysis—gravitate toward open-ended and unconfined forms of writing, from essays and fragments to paradoxes and postcards. Stanley Cavell turns to film criticism; Arthur Danto writes about modern art; and Alain Badiou translates, revises, and updates Plato's Republic. Such sideways endeavors, among their other attractions, allow thinkers and writers to assume the role of impromptu, accidental wanderers.

Notes

1 See Graeme D. Bird, "Ring Composition," in The Cambridge Guide to Homer, ed. Corinne Ondine Pache (Cambridge: Cambridge University Press, 2020), 199–200; and Daniel Mendelsohn, Three Rings: A Tale of Exile, Narrative, and Fate (Charlottesville: University of Virginia Press, 2020).

2 The Odyssey, trans. Emily Wilson (New York: Norton, 2018), 218 (VII.251).

3 Ludwig Wittgenstein, Philosophical Investigations (1953), ed. G. E. M. Anscombe and R. Rhees, trans. G. E. M. Anscombe, 2nd edn (Oxford: Blackwell, 1958), 49 (§123).

4 Friedrich Nietzsche, The Will to Power (1901), ed. Walter Kaufmann, trans. Walter Kaufmann and R. J. Hollingdale (New York: Random House, 1967), 291, 327 (§540 and §604). These notebook entries from 1883 to 1888 were published posthumously.

5 Martin Heidegger, "Logos (Heraklit, Fragment 50)," in Vorträge und Aufsätze (1954), 4th edn (Pfullingen: Günther Neske, 1978), 218: "*wenn es im Befremdlichen wander....*" My translation.

6 Gerald L. Bruns, Heidegger's Estrangements: Language, Truth, and Poetry in the Later Writings (New Haven, CT: Yale University Press, 1989), 183–184. See also Karsten Harries, "Language and Silence: Heidegger's Dialogue with Georg Trakl," boundary 2 4, no. 2 (1976): 494–511.

7 Jacques Derrida, "I'm Going to Have to Wander All Alone" (1995), trans. Leonard Lawlor, *Philosophy Today* 42, no. 1 (1998): 3–5. See also Gilles Deleuze, "Nomad Thought" (1973), trans. David B. Allison, in The New Nietzsche: Contemporary Styles of Interpretation, ed. David B. Allison (Cambridge, MA: MIT Press, 1985), 142–149.

22 Wandering Eros

Wandering attracts the erotic. People who fall out of love tend to wander, and people who fall in love tend to wander too. Freddy Eynsford-Hill in *My Fair Lady* (1964), walking down a familiar street where Eliza Doolittle lives, experiences an oxytocin-fuelled, lovestruck liftoff that resembles a sudden, involuntary vertical wander: "All at once am I several stories high…."[1] Hyperspace wandering and intergalactic time travel can even function "like a metaphor for sex," at least according to a popular book subtitled The Smart Bitches' Guide to Romance Novels.[2] Sex, however, is not identical with the erotic. French polymath theorist Georges Bataille describes the difference succinctly: "Sexual reproductive activity is common to sexual animals and men [*l'homme*]," he writes in 1957, "but only men appear to have turned their sexual activity into erotic activity."[3]

Erotic activity, unlike sex, depends upon what Bataille calls "the inner life" (*la vie intérieure*), and the inner life certainly finds room for almost every imaginable permutation of gender or gesture. The inner life can find a sonnet sequence erotic, or an email. It can turn Othello into a raging beast when he discovers a planted handkerchief, or it can melt with mysterious arousal at the passing scent of perfume. Hardcore pornography, by contrast, in depicting sexual acts may wholly fail to achieve the erotic. "Human eroticism," as Bataille nails down his basic contrast, "differs from animal sexuality precisely in this, that it calls inner life into play."[4]

Wandering takes many trajectories as it intersects with the varieties of erotic experience, but such trajectories always involve the inner life. Three trajectories can serve as placeholders here for the almost infinitely varied possible courses of erotic wandering: loss, risk, and catastrophe.

Loss has a general affinity with wandering, but the erotic introduces the likelihood of a more particular, even inevitable loss. Loss and

DOI: 10.4324/9781003255307-22

love are in fact often interpenetrating states, if not inseparable, and nowhere is their entanglement more basic to an art form than in the blues. The blues—as a distinctive musical genre—regularly features love, loss, and wandering as an inseparable trio. Mississippi bluesman John Lee Hooker, for example, traveled widely enough to suggest that wandering (while common among professional musicians) is all but built into the blues. Born in the Delta in 1917, he moved to Memphis in the 1930s, moved again to Detroit in 1943, recorded in Chicago during the 1960s, and eventually settled in San Francisco. Lost love does not so much *initiate* wandering as *infiltrate* wandering and fill it up with longing in his gravel-voiced classic "Wandering Blues" (c. 1950).

The blues, as an indigenous African American art, embraces a dark history of racism absent from most mainstream love songs.[5] Race thus imparts its own particular soulful signature on the wider musical repertoire of love, and Hooker's "Wandering Blues" is representative both in its Delta-inspired guitar riffs and in its focus on the inner life as filtered through the black experience of racism. The familiar unstable triangular geometry of Eros—lover, beloved, and rival—takes an unexpected turn in Hooker's version of the inner life, as the male lover is consumed in imagining his beloved not simply as lost or absent but as a woman with her own erotic trajectory and complicated inner life. It is a triangular asymmetry that in the blues is destined to result in wandering: "Every night I wander all by myself/ Thinkin' about the woman I love, *lovin' someone else*."[6]

Erotic wandering in Hooker's version also associates solitude with larger exclusions. The singer is excluded not only from love and from the inner life of the beloved but also from a social world that the blues, if indirectly, configures as racist. The bare lyrics on the page, then, tell a generic tale of lost love, but (filtered through the voice of John Lee Hooker) the blues also conveys the life experience of a world-weary, worn-out black survivor who already carries a load of pain. Billie Holiday's "Strange Fruit" (1939) makes this distinctive blues register unmistakable as her voice adds a haunting, incalculable sorrow. The multiple losses implicit in the blues cannot be eased simply by recovering the beloved. It is a loss that must be borne from song to song. Alone, as Hooker gives voice to a love affair gone wrong, wandering is not simply one option among many options. It is the inescapable default position when the personal losses implicit in Eros intersect with a collective history of racism.

Loss and wandering generate an equally distinctive partnership in the extensive erotic literature of leave-taking. The lover in Robert Burns's traditional Scottish folk song declares in the opening stanza that his love is as intense and pure as a newly opened ("red, red") rose. How can she resist? The lover continues to heap up erotic superlatives. The final stanza, however, changes everything:

And fare-thee-weel, my only Luve!
And fare-thee-weel a while!
And I will come again, my Luve,
Tho' 'twere ten thousand mile![7]

A conventional erotic song declaring love and praising the beloved suddenly turns on a dime. In promising to return, the lover is also, as the audience comes to understand, saying goodbye.

Loss in "My Luve's Like a Red, Red Rose" unfolds in multiple speech acts: a declaration of love, praise of the beloved, a farewell and, finally, a promise. The lover promises to return even if, in poet-speak, the distance is infinite ("ten thousand mile") and the journey endless (lasting until Judgment Day). The beloved is left behind, marinating in superlatives, implicitly asked to wait forever. How good is the lover's promise to return? Folk songs tell an all too familiar story about the woman who is left behind. The complicated layering of speech acts in a poem of such brief, stark simplicity suggests why Bob Dylan chose Burns's ballad when asked to name the lyric with the greatest impact on his life.[8] Dylan too is a master of erotic loss and wandering:

I'm walkin' down that long, lonesome road, babe
Where I'm bound, I can't tell
But goodbye's too good a word, gal
So I'll just say fare thee well….[9]

Farewells are not always gendered male, but often it is the male—whether left or leaving—who wanders. For once, in what helps make Ray Charles's "Hit the Road Jack" (1961) so distinctive, it is the woman who gets to say who will leave and who stays: "Hit the road Jack/ And don'cha come back/ No more, no more, no more, no more/ Hit the road Jack/ And don'cha come back no more…."[10]

Risk, as the second designated placeholder for erotic wandering, is folded into every romantic relationship, even if unacknowledged. Eros always entails the gamble that somebody, eventually, will hit the road, whether Jack or Jill. The romance novel today outsells all other categories of fiction and nonfiction, where women are not only heroines but also—most often—authors and readers. Most important, romance novels, while formulaic, also expand the possibilities open to modern women for taking on risk, especially risk that entails a likelihood of erotic wandering.

"Jeff and I traveled to eight countries in 21 days without changing clothes." This clickbait teaser appeared in a 2013 online article beneath an equally eye-catching title: "The craziest OkCupid date ever." It gets dizzying to count the tangled lines of genre and media crossed: romance novel, social network, autobiography, travel writing, adventure, advice column, and online dating. The web-based article caught enough eyeballs that Clara Bensen, who wrote the article and lived it, followed up three years later with a book-length memoir entitled No Baggage: A Minimalist Tale of Love and Wandering.[11]

"Do you have any ideas for travel experiments?" This is the fateful question that Jeff poses to Clara during their initial pre-date online chat. Jeff, no surprise, says that he intends to push "to the nth limit" his idea for an experiment: to fly overseas with no bags, no plan, and no itinerary. Arrival and departure points will be fixed—different, distant cities—with everything in between undetermined. Clara and Jeff have never met, but their tolerance for risk is a match. "We live for the unexpected, the experimental and the subtly disruptive," Clara explains. Off they go, barely six weeks after their first online contact, with little more than the clothes they wear, passports, and toothbrushes.

Cupid's blindness reflects the traditional view that lovers take big risks in taking leave of their senses. As they roll the dice, Clara and Jeff find that mutual risk-taking only enhances their growing attachment. Fortunately, it is a winning formula: "Our romantic relationship intact," concludes Clara, who writes up their adventure with a happy ending, "Jeff and I boarded the Heathrow return flight as closer friends than ever (despite the questionable state of our undergarments)." Clara as writer, by controlling the narrative and by infusing it with her wry humor, manages to achieve what the heroines of modern romance novels often pull off: she fully assumes the power to take charge of her own erotic risk-taking and its wandering outcomes.

Catastrophe, the final placeholder, describes what happens when loss and risk take a devastating turn toward chaos and utter collapse. Cupid ranks among the original erotic wanderers with the aid of sturdy wings and tricks that extend beyond comic mischief. Apuleius in The Golden Ass (c. 170–180 AD)—an early Latin romance—describes Cupid as "rampaging through people's houses at night armed with his torch and arrows, undermining the marriages of all."[12] The Latin *discurrens*, translated as "rampaging," means "running to and fro, roaming"—a reminder that Eros is given to wild, blind, tragic passions. It is Eros who, behind the scenes, helps transform the House of Atreus into a blood-soaked ruin.

Catastrophe lies beyond the carefully constructed screen that romance novels and pop songs promote with the truism that breaking up is hard to do. Breakups belong to the familiar bumpy course of love, which (as the lovers agree in A Midsummer Night's Dream) never did run smooth. Catastrophe, collapse, and ruin, however, are the volcanic eruptions reminding us that Eros can exact a terrible cost and that wandering, despite the happy landing for Clara and Jeff, often leads to fatal implosions. Hearts shatter forever and lives fall apart.

Martha Dickinson grew up in the same Amherst household with her now-famous aunt, whose manuscripts she published in 1914, helping to ignite the modern discovery of Emily Dickinson. Martha was also a poet, and in 1925 she titled her only published, book-length collection The Wandering Eros. The initial poem, "To Eros," begins ominously:

> With torch high held,
> A mounting flame
> Lifted above the envious enmity
> Of tempest
> Or of cloud—
> Eros the Wanderer strays.[13]

Straying—a synonym for wandering—attracts Cheryl Strayed to her new self-chosen surname, but it also invokes the distinctive bittersweetness of Eros, with bitterness often predominant. Martha Dickinson's choice of title is illuminated by the Emily Dickinson Museum website: "In 1902 while abroad in Bohemia, Martha married the romantic Alexander Bianchi, a captain in the Russian Imperial Horse Guards. He was later jailed on charges of fraud, and the couple separated in 1908, divorcing in 1920."[14] The torch-bearing, mischief-loving god Eros no doubt smiled and just wandered on.

The largest question may be whether wandering—except perhaps fugitive flight and exile—almost always includes erotic dimensions implicit in free, unconfined, risky wanderings on the open road of the inner life, with their renegade departures from everything staid, constraining, dull, and straight.

Notes

1 Alan Jay Lerner (lyrics) and Frederick Loewe (music), "On the Street Where You Live" (1956), https://genius.com/Frederick-loewe-on-the-street-where-you-live-lyrics.

2 Sarah Wendell and Candy Tan, Beyond Heaving Bosoms: The Smart Bitches' Guide to Romance Novels (New York: Simon & Schuster, 2009), 105. For a diagram of the traditional structure of romance novels, see Janice A. Radway, Reading the Romance: Women, Patriarchy, and Popular Literature (Chapel Hill: University of North Carolina Press, 1984), 150.

3 Georges Bataille, Erotism: Death and Sensuality (1957), trans. Mary Dalwood (San Francisco: City Lights Books, 1986), 11. The English translation was first published as Death and Sensuality: A Study of Eroticism and the Taboo (1962).

4 Bataille, Erotism, trans. Dalwood, 29.

5 See the classic study by Houston A. Baker, Jr., Blues, Ideology, and Afro-American Literature: A Vernacular Theory (Chicago: University of Chicago Press, 1984).

6 John Lee Hooker, "Wandering Blues," https://genius.com/John-lee-hooker-wandering-blues-lyrics. Italics added. The song (dated c. 1950) is recorded on his album John Lee Hooker Sings Blues (1960). On Hooker's life and music, see Robert Palmer, Deep Blues: A Musical and Cultural History, from the Mississippi Delta to Chicago's South Side to the World (New York: Viking Penguin, 1981), 242–246. On the triangular geometry of love, see Anne Carson, Eros the Bittersweet: An Essay (1986; rpt. Princeton: Princeton University Press, 2014).

7 Robert Burns, "A Red, Red Rose" (1794), http://robertburns.org/works/444.shtml. Burns gave the song to Italian singer Pietro Urbani for the six-volume collection A Selection of Scots Songs: Harmonized, Improved with Simple, and Adapted Graces (1792–1804). It is not known if Burns—a collector of Scottish folk songs—created, revised, or merely transcribed it.

8 Sean Michaels, "Bob Dylan: Robert Burns Is My Biggest Inspiration," *The Guardian*, 6 October 2008, https://www.theguardian.com/music/2008/oct/06/bob.dylan.robert.burns.inspiration.

9 Bob Dylan, "Don't Think Twice, It's All Right," https://www.bobdylan.com/songs/dont-think-twice-its-all-right. The song appeared on The Freewheelin' Bob Dylan (1963).

10 "Hit the Road Jack," https://genius.com/Ray-charles-hit-the-road-jack-lyrics. The song, written by Percy Mayfield, was first recorded by Ray Charles in 1961.

11 Clara Bensen, "The Craziest OkCupid Date Ever," *Salon*, 12 November 2013, https://www.salon.com/2013/11/12/the_craziest_okcupid_date_ever; and No Baggage: A Minimalist Tale of Love and Wandering (Philadelphia, PA: Running Press, 2016).

12 Apuleius, The Golden Ass, trans. P. G. Walsh (New York: Oxford University Press, 1994), 76 (IV.30).

13 Martha Dickinson Bianchi, The Wandering Eros (Cambridge, MA: Houghton Mifflin, 1925), xi.

14 "Martha Dickinson (Mattie) Bianchi (1886–1943), Niece," Emily Dickinson Museum, https://www.emilydickinsonmuseum.org/martha-dickinson-bianchi-1866-1943-niece.

23 Wandering and wondering

The war in Heaven comes to an abrupt end in Paradise Lost (1667) when God hurls Lucifer and his renegade angels headlong into the void. They tumble for nine days until finally landing in Hell on the infamous lake of fire. There Lucifer adopts his new name, Satan, rouses his troops, and begins plotting revenge. The fallen angels (now minor devils) meanwhile heave themselves off the burning lake, "wand'ring, each his several way…."[1] What occupies them? Some gather on a hill to reason about abstruse points of theology—but find no conclusion, "in wand'ring mazes lost" (II.561).

Paradise Lost establishes or at least vividly illustrates the paradigm for a theology of ambiguous wandering and wondering. The two distinct activities play a paired role, for better or for worse, which extends throughout the history of religious thought. Wandering and wondering can establish a fruitful partnership greatly enhancing religious or spiritual experience, but—as with Milton's minor devils debating the finer points of providence, foreknowledge, fate, and free will—they also constitute a pairing that, in its ambiguities and doubleness, can go endlessly, aridly, disastrously wrong.

Paradise Lost offers a Christian primer on the double life of wandering, both fallen and unfallen, which mirrors a related doubleness in wonder. The positive qualities of various serpentine patterns in the Garden of Eden reflect the prelapsarian innocence of Adam and Eve. The streams in Paradise curve gracefully "with mazy error" (IV.239) and with "serpent error wand'ring" (VII.302). The sinuous triplet "serpent error wand'ring" indicates that even serpents, in the prelapsarian garden, are still unfallen. After the Fall, however, serpents, mazes, error, and wandering all turn sinister. Eve's "wand'ring vanity" (X.875) is what Adam says led her to succumb to temptation, and curved forms always recall the satanic serpent with his waving coils and twisted

DOI: 10.4324/9781003255307-23

rhetoric. Wandering too in the postlapsarian world bears the fallen taint of sin and mortality.

Wandering in Milton's puritan, dissenting vision of a world fallen into sin reflects a deliberate departure from pagan theologies, where the Olympian gods (in their birthright as superhumans) wander wherever they please, with morals as loose as their flowing garments. No pagan god proved more footloose than Odin, often regarded as the supreme Germanic deity. In Norse mythology, he often appears (one-eyed) in his role as wanderer, complete with hat, cloak, and staff (Figure 23.1). The doubleness that he embodies is the uncanny and dangerous power that belongs to a god who disguises his superhuman powers in the deceptively powerless figure of a wanderer.

With two good eyes, Odin might pass for the kindly, retired pedlar in Wordsworth's Excursion, and he reappears as the Wanderer, for example, in Richard Wagner's *Ring* cycle (1876), where his power is waning but he remains still a godly force to reckon with. Also known as Wodin

Figure 23.1 After Georg von Rosen. *Odin, in his guise as a wanderer* (1886). Illustration from Fredrik Sander, Edda Sämund den Vises (1893).

or Wotan, he remains (even in the twilight of the deities) a Teutonic power of frenzy and poetic fervor: a Dionysian wanderer to be wary of.

Wotan as the wandering god of frenzy deeply troubled Carl Jung. Jung views ancient gods as archetypes of human psychic powers, and he saw Wotan-like psychic forces reflected in the rise of Hitler and in the German political chaos toward the end of the Weimar Republic. Both the man and the moment embodied, in Jung's view, the spirit of Wotan: the "restless wanderer (*rastlose Wanderer*) who creates unrest and stirs up strife." From the relative quiet of Switzerland, Jung is alarmed as the spirit of Wotan revives "like an extinct volcano." The ancient wanderer, in effect, redistributes his power among the restless German masses: "the wandering role was taken over by the thousands of unemployed, who were to be met with everywhere on their aimless journeys." Wandering, a favorite German outdoor pastime, had changed by 1933: "Wotan the wanderer was on the move."[2]

Wotan, in fact, makes a surprise appearance in a poem that Hitler composed as a young man: "I often go on bitter nights/ To Wotan's oak in the quiet glade/ With dark powers to weave a union…."[3] Jung's essay implies the need for extra vigilance as restless wandering shifts to a dangerous collective frenzy led by "a so-called Führer" (21). A few weeks after writing his poem, young Hitler tells his friends: "You will hear much about me. Just wait until my time comes."[4]

Wondering, while it can refer to simple puzzlement, also can share the double possibilities implicit in wandering. Wonders in Paradise Lost imply their traditional meaning of marvels, with the psychological astonishment they inspire, as when Milton describes the fallen angel-warriors as suddenly shrunk to pygmy size: "Behold a wonder!" (I.777). Paradise Lost soon becomes a prime example of what neoclassical critics call *le merveilleux chrétien*.[5] Wonder, however, as the emotional state inspired by marvels, can easily degenerate into idle or dangerous curiosity, which often ends in irresolution. Hamlet-like wondering, for example, occurs in a cognitive twilight state in which thinking—in the absence of certainties—simply loses its decisiveness, sidetracked in maybes. Wondering, however, in its more positive shapes is also compatible with chipping away at the unknown, slowly gaining confidence in twilight navigations, finding out direction from indirection, and occasionally even breaking through to astonishment.

The psychology of wandering—in its association with wonder—includes both enhanced attention (since wanderers don't know what to expect) and increased openness to the unexpected (since it occasionally produces daffodil-like experiences of wonder). Wondering, as a meditative state of cognition that never rises to the act of reasoning, nonetheless prepares the mind for lucky accidents. Luck favors the prepared mind, as Louis Pasteur observed—offering eureka moments when an encounter with apparently random accidents can lead to spiritual epiphanies or scientific discoveries, as when Alexander Fleming returned from holiday to find a bare spot in a petri dish, prelude to the life-saving invention of penicillin. Matthew Arnold, when he asserted bluntly that miracles do not happen, was referring specifically to an act of divine intervention that violates known laws of nature. What if, however, wandering and wondering in their kinship consist precisely in a redoubled openness that finds a new path to the miraculous?

It was in North Carolina during the heart of the Great Depression. The local police were preparing to run the Morgan family out of town. The Morgans, traveling evangelists, had camped for weeks in the town square, hanging their laundry on a Confederate monument and generally constituting what police call a public nuisance. Preacher Morgan pleaded for one more revival meeting, just to cover gas money. He had no idea that John Jacob Niles, a 41-year-old musician and folklorist, was employed nearby as personal assistant to a well-known photographer documenting folk arts in Appalachia. Niles, in turn, knew nothing about the Morgans. It was a collision of unknowns. Niles, as he wandered into a chance revival meeting, suddenly found what (without knowing it) he was looking for. For Niles, it was a moment of secular wonder.

A young girl—"a tousled, unwashed blond, and very lovely," as Niles wrote—stepped onto a little platform attached to the gas-poor Morgan family automobile. "Her clothes were unbelievably dirty and ragged," Niles noted, "and she, too, was unwashed. Her ash-blond hair hung down in long skeins…." Then, Annie Morgan began to sing. "She smiled as she sang," he recalled, "smiled rather sadly, and sang only a single line of a song."[6] A wonder had just occurred.

Gasoline in 1933 cost 18 cents a gallon.[7] Transfixed, Niles says he threw "a silver quarter" at her feet. She stopped singing. Afterward, he asked her to sing the entire song, again and again, eight repetitions at 25 cents each. He still managed to transcribe only three lines, plus notes. Wonder tends to defeat close analysis. The Morgans at least had their gas money, but Niles too had what he wanted. Within a year, he had reworked the lyrics, adding verses and music, publishing the results in his 1934 <u>Songs of the Hill-Folk</u>:

> I wonder as I wander out under the sky,
> How Jesus the Savior did come for to die.
> For poor on'ry people like you and like I...
> I wonder as I wander out under the sky.

Wandering and wondering have merged. Wondering, for poor ordinary—or is it ornery?—folk is an engagement with sacred mysteries: a wonder. How could a god descend from heaven and die to save poor ordinary people in rural North Carolina? Niles, an amateur musical prospector, knew he had stuck gold, and the song has long remained—far beyond its rural origins—a Christmas classic.

A Serious Way of Wondering (2003) is a nonfiction exploration of the ethics of Jesus by American novelist Reynolds Price. Price, a self-described "outlaw Christian," views Jesus as a divine figure inseparable from the mystery of the Resurrection.[8] It is a belief strengthened by what Price describes as his own "personal visionary experience of healing from a dire illness…" (115). Unlike the moral-rationalist Jesus of Thomas Jefferson, whose synoptic version of the New Testament omits all the miracles, the Jesus whom Price describes is a figure whose thought and life radiate a wondrous power.

Alexander Pope, with strong leanings toward an eighteenth-century reason-based ethics, never traveled outside England. He also preferred the Horatian imperative "wonder at nothing"—construed from Horace's famous Latin phrase *nil admirari*—as respecting the ancient philosophical preference for a life of calm contemplation. His well-known five-acre landscape garden adjacent to his Thames-side house in Twickenham served expressly as the setting for quiet, meditative reflection. It was an environment designed for wandering and pondering in a composed state that invited a deep connection with values and affections beyond the politics and economics of daily life.

Visitors entered Pope's flowing, natural garden through a long tunnel underneath the public road that separated his garden from the house. The passage, beginning with an ore-encrusted grotto, reflected a transition that assists the mind's transit into a state of meditation. The restricted entry and enclosed garden affirm both Pope's status as a private gentleman—removed from trade and court intrigue—and his preference for tranquil reflection. No matter where visitors wandered in the extended garden, its asymmetrical paths and perspectives were designed to embody variety and intricacy: principles soon widely adopted in a chiaroscuro, rough-edged, mottled landscape aesthetic called picturesque, which Pope deserves major credit for introducing into England. As visitors wander within the garden, its contours direct them ultimately toward its "visual and emotional climax": the obelisk that Pope erected to the memory of his mother.[9]

The obelisk is not a marvel, surely, not meant to inspire astonishment. Wonder, however, comes in many varieties. An obelisk set amid a picturesque landscape garden invites thoughts of vanished civilizations, human mutability, and a realm beyond earthly accomplishment. The Latin inscription begins "Ah Edith!" The elegiac "Ah"—a cry or sigh—precedes his mother's first name, her first name only, invoked in direct address and punctuated with an exclamation point. The inscription expresses Pope's filial devotion ("best of mothers") and singles her out ("most loved of women") as exceptional. Not a marvel but a meaningful, deliberate non-marvel, a sculptural remembrance or memorial, placed where its resonant final word—*Farewell*—invites a calm but emotion-rich moment for wondering.

Notes

1 John Milton, Paradise Lost (1667), ed. John Leonard (New York: Penguin Books, 2000), II.523. Further quotations are documented within the text. The first edition of Paradise Lost was divided into 10 books; these citations correspond to the 12-book division of the revised second edition (1674).
2 C. G. Jung, "Wotan" (1936), in Essays on Contemporary Events: The Psychology of Nazism, trans. R. F. C. Hull (1988; rpt. Princeton: Princeton University Press, 1989), 11–12. Further quotations are documented within the text. "On the move" translates *erwacht* (awakened)—as if a slumbering psychic force suddenly comes wide awake.
3 Quoted in John Toland, Adolf Hitler, 2 vols. (New York: Doubleday, 1976), I.68.
4 Toland, Hitler, I.68.
5 See David B. Morris, The Religious Sublime: Christian Poetry and Critical Tradition in 18th-Century England (Lexington: University Press of Kentucky, 1972), 39–44.
6 Quoted in Ron Pen, "I Wonder as I Wander," in A Kentucky Christmas, ed. George Ella Lyon (Lexington: University Press of Kentucky, 2003), 200. See also Ron Pen, I Wonder as I Wander: The Life of John Jacob Niles (Lexington: University Press of Kentucky, 2010).
7 US Office of Energy Efficiency & Renewable Energy, "Historical Gasoline Prices, 1929–2011," 20 August 2012, https://www.energy.gov/eere/vehicles/fact-741-august-20-2012-historical-gasoline-prices-1929-2011.
8 Reynolds Price, A Serious Way of Wondering: The Ethics of Jesus Reimagined (New York: Scribner, 2003), 114. Further quotations are documented within the text.
9 Maynard Mack, The Garden and the City: Retirement and Politics in the Later Poetry of Pope 1731–1743 (Toronto: University of Toronto Press, 1969), 28; and Morris R. Brownell, Pope and the Arts of Georgian England (Oxford: Clarendon Press, 1978), 71–145. The inscription reads: "*Ah Editha!/ Matrum optima./ Mulierum amantissima./ Vale.*"

24 A migratory species?

Are humans a migratory species? An unequivocal yes/no answer doesn't seem too much to ask for. Anthropologists, however, like to repeat an old joke that all of anthropology can be reduced to three statements, and the first two statements go like this: "It's all very complicated. Some do and some don't." (Statement number three concerns cultural relativism.) One group of experts, in 1998, was in no doubt about whether humans are a migratory species. "A careful examination of virtually any historical era," they write, "reveals a consistent propensity towards geographic mobility among men and women, who are driven to wander…." The experts continue confidently to sum up the evidence: "Like many birds, but unlike most other animals, humans are a migratory species."[1]

I respectfully await a definitive twenty-first-century statement, but meanwhile I would prefer to examine some of the complications. Although people and groups do in fact migrate, instances of human migration do not therefore prove that, logically or biologically, we are a migratory species. Humans do in fact skip rope. Are we therefore a rope-skipping species? Or do our brains simply permit a *capacity* for skipping rope, as well as for migrating? Of course, migration has possible survival value, unlike skipping rope, but it does not follow that we are genetically predisposed to migrate. Migration may be a simple byproduct of the brain-based capacity to move about and change location.

A capacity to migrate, not a gene or genetic network, may be as much as we can assert about what drives large-scale human relocations. Ancient tradition defined humans as rational animals. Jonathan Swift, surveying the evidence of human irrationality, decided that humans are not rational animals but only animals "capable" of reason: *rationis capax*.[2] Humans are certainly *capable* of migrating. We are also, however, unlike some birds, equally capable of *not* migrating.

DOI: 10.4324/9781003255307-24

Similarly, while we are capable of wandering, we are also equally capable of *not* wandering. Wanderers, like migrants, often conclude their movements by arriving at a new home, where they stop and (as we say in directional metaphors) settle down and put down roots. They do not necessarily possess a biological equivalent to whatever genetic codes impel northern geese to fly south for the winter.

Human migration, like wandering, is not always the wisest course of action. Our distant cousins *Homo erectus* walked or wandered out of Africa about 1.75 million years ago, not knowing they would hit a genetic dead end: migrating or wandering did not serve them well. *Homo sapiens* luckily staged their own migration much later, and by 40,000 BCE our ancestors had spread across Australia, Asia, and Europe. An ability to wander widely no doubt helped early *Homo sapiens* in Europe replace the sedentary Neanderthals. Humans as a species have migrated and wandered all over. It's how we ended up wherever we are right now. This fact, however, does not transform us into a migratory species like monarch butterflies or black woodpeckers.

Migration as an adaptive strategy at times certainly proves successful, but it can also prove (as for *Homo erectus*) disastrous. Staying put has also proved a successful adaptive strategy, although it too can lead to disaster. It's all very complicated. Some wander and some don't. An optional 1,100-mile hike on the Pacific Crest Trail increases the risk of death exponentially. Why would a well-evolved brain let us pull off such a stunt? If no gene or network of genes predisposes humans to migrate or wander, then we wanderers, secret or open, are on our own. We can't pin our crazy hikes, bad holidays, and home-shifting misadventures on Charles Darwin.

Wandering as a sign and consequence of brain damage in dementia patients suggests that the human brain, in ordinary working condition, prefers that we *not* wander. The panic that many people experience on getting lost suggests that the brain wants us to find our way home. We all carry traces of sedentary Neanderthal DNA, with exact percentages depending on our heritage.[3] Moreover, we share 98.5% of our DNA with chimpanzees. Chimps are known to migrate only as a last resort but otherwise live within small groups in well-defined territories. Does this sound like anyone you know?

Human health depends on complex interrelations between our personal biology and what we now call social determinants: human-caused conditions and group behaviors that influence health and illness, from asthma and some cancers to sex in the age of AIDS. Migration and wandering may be similarly open to the influence of social determinants. Climate change, terrorism, corruption, famine, war, pollution, and the fossil fuel industry all constitute specific social determinants that profoundly influence both health and wandering. A severe drought in Canaan is what drives the biblical patriarch Jacob to bring his family and flocks into Egypt, much as a tyrannical Pharaoh is what drives Moses to lead the Israelites *out* of Egypt. Both the drought and the Pharaoh constitute social determinants of wandering and migration. A potato blight, due to a microscopic fungus-like organism and benighted British policies, kills over a million people in Ireland from 1845 to 1852—driving another million to immigrate to the US. Social determinants are what tell people at certain points in human history to hit the open road, despite the perils ahead. We migrate or wander when times get tough because that's what humans, unlike black woodpeckers, just do.

The worldwide statistics are clear.[4] Across centuries and across cultures, the vast majority of humans stay put. Every refugee, migrant, pilgrim, nomad, and wanderer leaves behind an unofficial army of deep-rooted homebodies. Carl Sagan may be right that humans began as wanderers, and DNA analysis now allows scientists to track the movement of specific gene pools out of Africa, but wandering as an historical and cultural human practice remains relatively uncommon, and its uncommonness is what makes wandering—as opposed to staying home and watching television or playing video games—such a fascinating, unpredictable human practice.

There is always, of course, the option of consulting your local anthropologist about the third statement that completes the sum of anthropological knowledge, which perhaps holds the secret to migration and wandering. Apparently, there is as yet no unequivocal answer to the question of whether humans are a migratory species. It seems likely that we are not genetically programmed to migrate, although I await an authoritative pronouncement from biological anthropologists. They might, while they're at it, have a crack at why humans wander. The answer, again, may have less to do with genetics alone than with the bio-psychology of human curiosity.[5] Unlike migratory polar bears, who make annual and seasonal north-south treks, humans seem ready (as an inherently curious species?) to wander off—as the nursery rhyme tells us about the bear who went over the mountain—just to see what we can see. Or are we mistaken both about humans and bears?

Notes

1 Douglas S. Massey, Joaquín Arango, Graeme Hugo, Ali Kouaouci, Adela Pellegrino, and J. Edward Taylor, "New Migrations, New Theories," in

Worlds in Motion: Understanding International Migration at the End of the Millennium (Oxford: Oxford University Press, 1998), 1.

2 Jonathan Swift to Alexander Pope (29 September 1725), in The Correspondence of Jonathan Swift, ed. Harold Williams, 5 vols. (Oxford: Clarendon Press, 1963–1965), III.102–103.

3 Nathaniel Scharping, "How Much Neanderthal DNA Do Humans Have?," *Discover Magazine*, 28 April 2020, https://www.discovermagazine.com/planet-earth/how-much-neanderthal-dna-do-humans-have. See also Adam Clark Estes, "It Wasn't Just Neanderthals: Ancient Humans Had Sex with Other Hominids," *The Atlantic*, 6 September 2011, https://www.theatlantic.com/technology/archive/2011/09/it-wasnt-just-neanderthals-ancient-humans-had-sex-other-hominids/338117/.

4 "The Truth About Migration: We're a Stay-at-Home Species," *New Scientist*, 6 April 2016, https://www.newscientist.com/article/mg23030680-900-the-truth-about-migration-were-a-stayathome-species.

5 Celeste Kidd and Benjamin Y. Hayden, "The Psychology and Neuroscience of Curiosity," *Neuron* 88, no. 3 (2015): 449–460.

25 Leaving home

"And who are you?" the French border official asks Tristram Shandy. Tristram's reply? "Don't puzzle me."[1]

Wandering often starts with leaving home, and leaving home in the modern world regularly initiates questions of identity: a process of discovering who we are or will be. Ancient Greeks, who had a distinctive term (*nostos*) for the rite of homecoming, apparently had no corresponding term for leaving home. The departure from home, as in the nineteenth-century *Bildungsroman*, is a distinctively modern ritual associated with self-education and self-creation, and it often enlists an inexperienced, provincial figure who travels to the city. The plots feature a transition from innocence to experience. Leaving home in my family meant going off to college—not just going, but going *off*. A college education didn't preclude returning home, for brief periods, but it was understood as a transition to adult status, and it mostly signified that my room was up for grabs. Wandering, by contrast, was not the sign of a successful entry into much of anything.

Leaving home, once a required first step for younger sons seeking their fortune, is still an almost indispensable stage in wandering. Home in Richard Price's coming-of-age novel The Wanderers (1974) is not a house but a region, the Bronx, from which a small gang of Italian-American teen pals eventually, as life deals them different hands, wander away. Home, however, can also seem to wander away from you—or vanish in urban renewal or in wartime catastrophes, which initiate a different form of wandering, not quite exile but an irreversible exclusion. Home and the open road both turn dystopian in the *Mad Max* quartet of films (1979–2015), when social collapse transforms Australia into a bleak post-apocalyptic landscape against which the hero—his family murdered—abandons police work for a drifter's life of revenge that mostly calls upon him to destroy inventively armored vehicles driven at super high speed by inventively armored foes.

DOI: 10.4324/9781003255307-25

Everyone is a wanderer in science fiction sagas, it seems. There are still identifiable heroes and villains; duels must be fought and fathers slain. Evil empires or their dark surrogates, however, routinely pulverize homes and even home planets. In the absence of home, post-human habitation (shared with droids, replicants, cyborgs, and mutant humanoid creatures) shifts to wandering space-based battle stations as vast and inhospitable as floating nuclear power plants. Home—toxic, dysfunctional, or just plain vanished—is not what it used to be, certainly not like the Bronx in the early 1960s, and the survival of humans as a species (not just bedrooms or identities) now seems up for grabs.

Laurence Sterne, on the road in France, remains puzzled. Writing not as Tristram Shandy but in his transparent Shandean persona as Yorick, he complains, "There is not a more perplexing affair in life to me, than to set about telling any one who I am—for there is scarce any body I cannot give a better account of than of myself; and I have often wish'd I could do it in a single word—and have an end of it."[2] There is no end, however, to the questions of personal identity set in motion by wandering. Leaving home is the signal for initiating a proliferation of unending questions about who exactly we think we are.

Fictional accounts of leaving home frequently raise questions that turn increasingly difficult in an era when both homes and identities prove ambiguous. Whose home? Which identities? Homeless children in the US (according to summary figures for 2013) typically live with an African American mother who is under the age of 27. Domestic violence and sexual abuse are widespread among such women, with 90% victims of severe trauma. Young mothers already struggling with trauma and with the demands of childcare, often poorly educated, face few attractive opportunities to earn a living wage. Can they even afford the childcare that might let them hold a steady job?[3] Children miss supportive rituals and routines as they deal with divorce, evictions, foster care, living with relatives, motel hopping, sleeping in cars, and bouncing among schools. "You always dream about living in a house with your children," says a young Honduran mother speaking from a bus station in Brownsville, Texas, after crossing the US–Mexico border with her six-year-old daughter. "Now we have nothing."[4]

Archetypes of the wanderer today need to include a woman of color and her young child, with no home, little hope, uncertain where their next meal will come from. They are the Unseen Wanderers for whom questions of identity are less urgent than questions of survival.

Singularities can prove as revealing as archetypes when each wanderer traces out a distinctive path. Recently, I wondered if I could recall all the homes I've lived in. The first six homes didn't count since I was bundled like luggage as the Army moved my parents around. My amended list ultimately extends to 20 homes in 12 states. (I was astonished to find all 20 still visible on Google Earth.) Americans are a mobile lot, with an average 11.4 lifetime moves.[5] Europeans average four lifetime moves, so leaving home likely entails different experiences across the Atlantic Ocean. In Central America, migrant children often travel with their parents—or sometimes are entrusted to smugglers—only to wait in endless queues at the US border as politicians debate their futures. Migrants from northern Africa and the Middle East risk death at sea—not just any old risk—to slip into Europe. We may all soon have to rethink our identities as wanderers or as future fellow wanderers.

Leaving home nonetheless remains an unnamed Western rite of passage. "Ever since I was a child," begins rock star Ray Davies, "I loved to wander wild/ Through the bright city lights/ And find myself a life I could call my own." The lyrics—from the song "Life on the Road" (1977) by the The Kinks—describe the wanderings of a musician whose life on the road also includes a dream of returning home ("one of these days"). His desire for a homecoming, however, gets overpowered by a final, affirmative, contrary refrain: "Give me life on the road./ I said life on the road."[6] Two competing desires play out—wandering and homecoming—as the music ultimately reaffirms a life of moving on, as if the road holds an addictive quality or as if life on the road is inseparable from life itself. Is wandering ultimately a concealed figure or metaphor for living?

Samuel Johnson once wrote, in his voice as a moral philosopher, "The business of life is to go forwards…."[7]

Wandering, as a *going forwards*, implicitly assigns the highest value and greatest good to the act of movement. Forwards is not a direction but a motion. Everything else, including questions of identity, takes second position. A practical wisdom suggests that certain questions can be left unsettled, which means at least they are not settled wrongly. Wandering does not necessarily lead to clarifications about personal identity, especially a selfhood somehow singular and coherent, fixed rather than, say, mixed, mixed up, and continually in flux. Native American poet, video artist, and filmmaker Sky Hopinka recognizes that his personal identity is inseparable from his tribal identity, and neither can simply exclude his status as born in the US.[8] "As much as I am confounded by the idea of being American in addition to being Ho-Chunk and Pechanga," he says in an interview, "I am still part of this landscape." Place too adds abiding complications to identities that wandering cannot promise to clarify. Hopinka's personal relocation to the Midwest marks his return to a place where, oddly, he had never set foot: "my tribe is from Wisconsin, so it was also a homecoming for me."[9] Homecomings are easier to recognize than unnamed rituals of leaving home because we know when they occur. Much as homes are no longer unambiguous places, it is not always clear when leaving home occurs, what it may mean, or whether walking out the door with no plan except going forwards will end in a love-hate relationship with wandering.

Leaving home, as a modest modern rite of passage, differs from homecoming precisely by virtue of its blurry margins. A homecoming, whenever it occurs, at least has the character of an event: an Odyssean circuit has been completed. There are greetings, speeches, or quiet reunions. Leaving home, by contrast, is often a nonevent. It just happens, perhaps early one morning, with no parades or speeches, maybe a tearful goodbye, but of course you'll be back soon, so no worries. Write or call! Leaving home rarely has the clarity of a door slammed shut, permanent exile, or a one-way ticket. What kind of event is it if you don't recognize it when it occurs? Leaving home, as an action, is less like an event than like catching the flu. You are going about the business of going forwards when suddenly you are somewhere else, or in the middle of something, or down with a cold. It's all so indefinite, with the character of a fuzzy, drifting, extended nonhappening. Wandering erodes the lines of demarcation that identify when it begins and how it changes you in ways that likely you too don't recognize and can't fully understand.

"In three days, I will be homeless," writes Brianna Karp. She is beginning a blog—a distinctly postmodern digital enterprise—which eventually leads to her book-length memoir The Girl's Guide to Homelessness (2011). She is 23 and suddenly jobless as she leaves her current home. Two years later, her book appears, ending happily, as she notes that she has just started "an amazing job at a prestigious Orange County theatre…." She has also discovered a purpose and a sense of belonging, which she describes as an activist's role in lending her newfound voice to support the homeless. "All my life I've longed for someplace to call my own," she adds, "—and not just a physical building, but a niche, somewhere that I fit in and feel a sense of harmony and *belonging*."[10]

Fernweh. Many wanderers share a desire to feel a sense of belonging, but wandering cannot promise the sense of emotional homecoming that Brianna Karp achieves. She has managed to close a circle, or open a new circle, but for many wanderers there is no closure, no circle to close, and nothing but the road ahead, stretching into darkness.

Identities remain fixed, confused, or in flux. Even the fellowship of the road is mostly interruptive, unsteady, and so thin at times as to seem illusory. The campfire circle of elderly van-dwellers often breaks up with the wanderers exchanging a standard euphemism: "See you down the road." Maybe so. Probably not.

Notes

1 Laurence Sterne, Tristram Shandy, ed. Howard Anderson (New York: Norton, 1980), 369 (vol. 7, chapter xxxiii).
2 Laurence Sterne, A Sentimental Journey Through France and Italy by Mr. Yorick (1768) (New York: Penguin, 2001), 82.
3 See Ellen L. Bassuk, Carmela J. DeCandia, Corey Anne Beach, and Fred Berman, America's Youngest Outcasts: A Report Card on Homelessness, American Institutes for Research, November 2014, https://www.air.org/sites/default/files/downloads/report/Americas-Youngest-Outcasts-Child-Homelessness-Nov2014.pdf.
4 Catherine E. Shoichet, "Two Big Factors Are Making Things Worse at the Border. But They're Not Getting Much Attention," *CNN*, 24 March 2021, https://www.cnn.com/2021/03/24/us/border-climate-change-covid/index.html.
5 Mona Chalabi, "How Many Times Does the Average Person Move?," *FiveThirtyEight*, 29 January 2015, https://fivethirtyeight.com/features/how-many-times-the-average-person-moves. Figures are based on the 2007 census.
6 The Kinks, "Life on the Road," https://genius.com/The-kinks-life-on-the-road-lyrics. Written by Ray Davies, the song appears in the album *Sleepwalker* (1977).
7 Samuel Johnson, The Idler No. 72 (1 September 1759), in Selected Essays from the *Rambler, Adventurer*, and *Idler*, ed. W. J. Bate (New Haven, CT: Yale University Press, 1968), 344.
8 Mariána Fernandez, "For Sky Hopinka, Wandering Is Both a Mode of Moving and Making," *Hyperallergic*, 10 February 2021, https://hyperallergic.com/621007/sky-hopinka-bard-review-centers-of-somewhere.
9 "Resisting Exploitation: Sky Hopinka Interviewed by Osman Can Yerebakan," *Bomb Magazine*, 24 September 2018, https://bombmagazine.org/articles/resisting-exploitation-sky-hopinka-interviewed/.
10 Brianna Karp, The Girl's Guide to Homelessness: A Memoir (New York: Harlequin, 2011), 3, 333–334.

26 The end of the road

I've been wanderin' early and late
From New York City to the Golden Gate
And it don't look like
I'm ever gonna cease my wanderin'....

—Anonymous American folk song[1]

Wandering often seems endless and irrational, which adds to the mystery of why it happens at all. *The end* is an illusion, however, a phantasm of linear thinking, as Jean Baudrillard argues.[2] Events stop but rarely conclude. Suppose that moving on is all we ever do; endlessness is all there is; and wandering simply exposes the fallacy of endings. Fifteen Asian elephants in 2021 wandered across China in a yearlong trek.[3] Nobody knows why. The headline term *wandering* is, of course, an anthropocentric projection, which assumes elephants act like humans. Ludwig Wittgenstein famously imagined that if lions could talk, we couldn't understand what they have to tell us.[4] Can we understand the elephants? If not, wandering may still be the best metaphor available. The elephants appear to have no destination, only a general northward direction. Becky Shu Chen, consultant for the Zoological Society of London and an expert on elephant-human interactions, says, "It makes me think of the movie 'Nomadland.'"[5]

Human wandering is as mysterious as whatever was happening to the elephants. In A Thousand Plateaus (1980), philosopher Gilles Deleuze and psychotherapist Félix Guattari come closest to creating a theory of wandering in their distinction between *nomadic* and *sedentary* orders. The terms—developed in their two-volume study of capitalism and schizophrenia—refer to how people live in relation to land. The sedentary relationship exemplified in farms or in nation-states might be described as (my addition) like an occupation. Sedentary people, like an invading army, *occupy* the land. They take possession

DOI: 10.4324/9781003255307-26

of it—engaged in specific trades, professions, and *occupations*—and they build permanent structures to work and to defend the land they occupy. Nomadic people, by contrast, do not so much occupy or possess the land as move *across* it. They are perpetually in between stops. "The life of the nomad," as Deleuze and Guattari depict this in-betweenness with a musical metaphor, "is the intermezzo."[6]

A theoretical contrast between nomadic and sedentary orders, while useful for thought, has the limitation of binaries that fail to account for hybrids, outliers, future developments, and the complexities of historical practice. The contrast wobbles when applied to current political events, such as struggles to create post-national identities for the multilingual citizens of a relatively new EU.[7] Jawbreakers such as *territorialization, deterritorialization*, and *reterritorialization* open beautiful vistas for thought, but what do we make of a person who is neither nomadic nor sedentary but, perhaps like Melville's Bartleby the Scrivener, prefers to resist either/or states of being? John Barth's comic novel The End of the Road (1958) begins with Jacob Horner sitting immobile for 24 hours in Penn Station, as if paralyzed by his inability to choose a destination. His motionlessness puts him outside both the sedentary and nomadic orders, while his expensive attire and suitcase protect him, he says, from police attention as a "vagrant."[8] They also define his distance from a truly nomadic order, just as his immobility (on a bench in a train station) is not truly sedentary. His condition embodies an episodic anomaly, and a therapist eventually reels him back in to everyday life with the arbitrary instruction to get a job.

Wanderers too may share a temporary Horner-like indecision and outsider status. Not easily confined, even in the intermezzo, wanderers may just wander outside the theater, skip the second act, go for a smoke, surf the web, or simply refuse to budge until something or someone forces them to get moving again.

Wandering, in short, is a native outlier. It may not signal a choice between binaries but rather the search for a way out. Wandering, neither the intermezzo nor the opera, may instead gesture toward the exit. Must we choose between a sedentary order of climate-roasting megacities and perpetual movement across borders now hardened with checkpoints and defensive firepower? The Asian elephants, in their exit from the Xishuangbanna National Nature Reserve, may simply heed an impulse to resist the orders that humans established to confine and protect them.

The English word *planet*—drawn from another human-established order—derives from an ancient Greek root that means "to wander."

Planet initially referred to the seven visible celestial bodies in our solar system that, unlike fixed stars, appear to wander. Only in the seventeenth century did *planet* come to designate the celestial bodies orbiting the sun. Planets, as we now know, do not wander. Lost dogs may wander and people do wander, but not planets. Today, oddly, we know more about the planets in our solar system—including the demotion of Pluto in 2006 to the status of a mere *dwarf planet*—than we know about terrestrial wandering.

Wandering, as a human practice varying across times and cultures, resists all efforts to extract a single, clear, and distinct underlying quality or essence. Social usage keeps changing, and there is simply no changeless mode of speech or thought that will define wandering for all time. No absolute law or rule exists to distinguish motionless, dreamlike drift from wandering through Paris on foot. Wandering is a higgledy-piggledy phenomenon: you can wander in a circle, on the high seas, standing still, or dancing with the daffodils. There is no mold or model that fits every wanderer, no way to distinguish genuine wanderers from frauds who only appear to wander. Can robots wander? Delivery robots can get stuck in the snow, so might they also wander off? No doubt hackers or renegade programmers are eager to intervene. Humans can wander for 40 years or 40 minutes, maybe even 40 seconds, as if in brief mind-wandering catnaps. Alpha waves may distinguish wandering from related modes of consciousness, such as meditation, but there is not even a requisite intention: you can wander by plan, by chance, or just by drifting along with the tumbling tumbleweeds.

Tristram Shandy shows that a novel can wander as easily as a person, especially a person given to digressions. Wandering often overlaps with the deviant, heterodox, contrary, crooked, transgressive, boundary-crossing, shape-shifting, paradoxical, and uncontainable. Small wonder that the police and public authorities seek to contain it or declare it illegal. It embraces the unembraceable in logic-defying contortions. Andy Warhol famously asserted that art is what you can get away with. Wandering too is an art of what you can get away with while you are engaged in going forward.

Wandering can also represent a counter-ethos opposed to capitalist labor and to instrumental reason. It doesn't pay, won't listen to reason, and never accomplishes much of anything. "I loafe and invite my soul," Whitman writes, as if rejecting the life of "quiet desperation" that Thoreau saw among his industrious New England neighbors.[9] The daffodils that Wordsworth's speaker suddenly encounters beside the lake matter less as external objects—which is their status in the neoclassical poetry of natural description—than as a source of internal shifts in mind and mood, a kind of daffodil therapy:

> A poet could not but be gay,
> In such a jocund company....[10]

Wandering cannot promise awe-inspiring views like the vistas in brochures put out by the travel and tourist industry: sightseeing prizes, like a glimpse of the aurora borealis. Daffodils may have to suffice. Feelings too wander in sync with the changing arc of our wanderings. "Our moods do not believe in each other," Emerson writes, describing emotional inconsistencies that run parallel to our self-contradictions.[11] Wanderers are connoisseurs of shifting moods and emotions. "Feelin' good was easy," as Janis Joplin sings about hitchhiking with Bobby McGee. Singing the blues, like Bobby McGee, or just aimlessly rounding a blind turn in a path, wanderers may stumble upon a sight that takes the breath away—and that stays with them, for years and decades afterward, as Janis Joplin works out the calculus of wandering: "I'd trade all of my tomorrows for one single yesterday...."

Aimlessness translates the Sanskrit term *apranihita*: meaning, literally, that a person "places nothing in front."[12] In certain schools of Buddhist meditation, it refers to the inner life of a person who makes no plans, who holds no hopes, and who entertains no desires. With nothing in front, disciples who practice *apranihita* often engage in the practice of "aimless wandering." Its aim, if such a Western concept makes sense, is to free the practitioner from anxieties and to permit an experience of "pure being." Classically trained musician Stephen Nachmanovitch performs concerts with no score, no plan, and no idea of what he will play on stage. He describes such improvisational aimlessness as belonging to "the art of is."[13]

Plato and Aristotle taught outdoors, while walking, and they equated thinking and walking with reasoning (as a progression of logical steps).[14] Wandering seeks no progressions. It prefers to digress. It seems unreasonable—or at least doesn't make sense—to sensible, reasonable people. Much as thinking or cognition, however, consists in more than logical reasoning, wandering preserves a fidelity to thought as colored with feeling, memory, and the nonconscious life of the body, less like a progression of (logical) steps than like the experience of a rainbow or the early morning odor of fresh-brewed coffee. Wandering, in this register, is like a thought that refuses to emerge fully into language. In an age of identity politics, it resists full disclosure. Indeed, just when you think you have corralled wandering and trapped it within a set of airtight, rational propositions—boxed it in, wrestled it into submission, and taken its full measure—it more or less slips away, as it always does, and just wanders off.

Wandering, in its unphilosophical preference for improvisation, most resembles a form of play. Hide-and-seek, a game invented by kids for kids, identifies the winner as the person who simply manages to stay out of sight. It has no clock and no scoreboard. When adults wander, they may temporarily regain a freedom from adult responsibilities, adult schedules, and adult rules. Just stay out of sight so no one can find you. It is wildly immature.

Suffering, unfortunately, is not something that wanderers can entirely avoid through playful improvisation. It is human suffering that sets Siddhartha Gautama on his journey. Significantly, his wanderings are not what bring enlightenment. Siddhartha finds enlightenment only when he stops wandering and sits still, immobile, under the Bodhi tree. There, he enters a frame of being distinct from either the sedentary or nomadic orders. For the Buddha, much as for Odysseus, wandering reaches its limit, exhausts its resources, completes its task, and comes to a halt. For others, especially for individuals caught in Cain-like cycles of endless affliction, wandering seems perpetual, home is unattainable, there is no task, no completion, and we wander because we can't stop wandering.

"The soul, uneasy and confin'd from home," writes Alexander Pope in An Essay on Man (1733–1734), "Rests and expatiates in a life to come."[15] What does it mean to *expatiate* in a life to come? *Expatiate*, according to Samuel Johnson's Dictionary of the English Language (1755), means "to range at large; to rove without any prescribed limits." Or, as Merriam-Webster defines it: "to move about freely, to wander."

A wandering that is open-ended and without purpose—restless, aimless, or simply unconfined—does not necessarily offer solace or consolation for suffering, but it also makes no demands. Thoreau sets the bar high for walkers. "If you are ready to leave father and mother, and brother and sister, and wife and child and friends, and never see them again," he writes; "if you have paid your debts, and made your will, and settled all your affairs, and are a free man; then you are ready for a walk."[16] Few walkers, I suspect, will accept Thoreau's challenge. I admire the talk, with its rhetoric of spiritual pilgrimage, but I am not prepared to walk the walk. Wandering is, compared with Thoreau's expectation of walkers, less transcendental and more human-scale. It does not seek to change the world or to change you. Certainly, its quietist outlook remains open to criticism. *Agendas*—from the Latin *agere* ("to do")—are what it deliberately avoids. Wandering is less an action than a way of inhabiting the world without agendas, objects of desire, designs, or marketplace aspirations. Its extreme lack of agendas suggests a preference for a Rilke-like surreptitious and invisible life of secrecy.

Wandering at its vanishing point gestures toward disappearance, absence, and self-effacement, as if it attains visibility mainly in fleeting traces of departure that it leaves behind (Figure 26.1).

Traces and absence may seem unduly elegiac—a return to the Wanderer as Anglo-Saxon exile or to Pope's obelisk—but, in a positive twist, they offer a strange kind of belonging: not local, not here nor there, but impersonal and widely diffused: mobile, fluid, unfixed, as common as air or water. "I bequeath myself to the dirt to grow from the grass I love," writes Whitman on his perpetual tramp: "If you want me again, look for me under your boot-soles."[17]

As Adam and Eve face immediate expulsion from the Garden of Eden, Paradise Lost evokes a deep and wide sense of loss—loss of Paradise, loss of direct communion with God, loss of the mutual trust between wedded partners—but Milton also softens the losses in the final two lines:

> They hand in hand with wand'ring steps and slow,
> Through Eden took their solitary way.[18]

Figure 26.1 Footsteps in the Sahara Desert. Morocco. Photo: Erg Chebbi. Stocksy.

Wand'ring steps and slow: this is the future pace and fate of humankind, Milton implies. Adam and Eve in their solitude—cut off from direct communion with God, estranged even from the animals, and headed into an unknown future—need each other more than ever. Their union "hand in hand" suggests that a Miltonic doubleness within wandering (fallen and unfallen) might yield to a third outcome: wandering as the human condition—but with its burdens softened, if we are lucky, by the companionship of a fellow wanderer.

Notes

1 "I've been wanderin'" dates from the early 1900s, with no known author.

2 Jean Baudrillard, The Illusion of the End (1992), trans. Chris Turner (Stanford: Stanford University Press, 1994). For another approach, see Frank Kermode, The Sense of an Ending: Studies in the Theory of Fiction (1967; rpt. New York: Oxford University Press, 2000).

3 John Ruwitch, "Elephants Wandered Hundreds of Miles Into a Chinese City. Nobody Knows Why," *NPR*, 4 June 2021, https://www.npr.org/2021/06/04/1003268230/elephants-wandered-hundreds-of-miles-into-a-chinese-city-nobody-knows-why.

4 Ludwig Wittgenstein, Philosophical Investigations (1953), ed. G. E. M. Anscombe and R. Rhees, trans. G. E. M. Anscombe, 2nd edn (Oxford: Blackwell, 1958), 223.

5 Quoted in Vivian Wang, "15 Chinese Elephants Are on a Long March North. Why, No One Knows," *New York Times*, 5 June 2021, https://www.nytimes.com/2021/06/03/world/asia/china-elephants.html.

6 Gilles Deleuze and Félix Guattari, A Thousand Plateaus: Capitalism and Schizophrenia (1980), trans. Brian Massumi (Minneapolis: University of Minnesota Press, 1987), 380.

7 On the politics of a new transnational identity, see Rosi Braidotti, Nomadic Theory: The Portable Rosi Braidotti (New York: Columbia University Press, 2011), especially her chapter "Nomadic European Citizenship" (239–264).

8 John Barth, The End of the Road (1958; rpt. McLean, IL: Dalkey Archive Press, 2016), 74.

9 Walt Whitman, "Song of Myself," in Leaves of Grass (1855), ed. David S. Reynolds (New York: Oxford University Press, 2005), 1; Henry David Thoreau, Walden (1854), ed. Jeffrey S. Cramer (New Haven, CT: Yale University Press, 2004), 7.

10 William Wordsworth, "I Wandered Lonely as a Cloud" (1807), in The Collected Poems of William Wordsworth (Ware, Hertfordshire: Wordsworth Editions Limited, 1994) ll.15–16.

11 "Circles" (1841), in Essays by Ralph Waldo Emerson, Introduction by Irwin Edman (1926; rpt. New York: Harper Perennial, 1951), 216. This single volume contains both the First Series (1841) and Second Series (1844).

12 Dan Lusthaus, Buddhist Phenomenology: A Philosophical Investigation of Yogācāra Buddhism and the *Ch'eng Wei-shih Lun* (London: Routledge, 2002), 266.

13 Stephen Nachmanovitch, The Art of Is: Improvising as a Way of Life (Novato, CA: New World Library, 2019).
14 Emily Thomas, "Five Philosophers on the Joys of Walking," *OUPblog*, 16 February 2020, https://blog.oup.com/2020/02/five-philosophers-on-the-joys-of-walking.
15 Alexander Pope, An Essay on Man (1733–1734), in The Poems of Alexander Pope, ed. John Butt (New Haven, CT: Yale University Press, 1963), i.97–i.98.
16 Henry D. Thoreau, "Walking" (1862), in Excursions, ed. Joseph J. Moldenhauer (Princeton: Princeton University Press, 2007), 186.
17 Whitman, "Song of Myself," in Leaves of Grass, ed. Reynolds, 44.
18 John Milton, Paradise Lost (1667), ed. John Leonard (New York: Penguin Books, 2000), XII.648–649. The first edition of Paradise Lost was divided into 10 books; this citation corresponds to the 12-book divison of the revised second edition (1674).

Name & Title Index

For Product Safety Concerns and Information please contact our EU
representative GPSR@taylorandfrancis.com
Taylor & Francis Verlag GmbH, Kaufingerstraße 24, 80331 München, Germany

www.ingramcontent.com/pod-product-compliance
Lightning Source LLC
LaVergne TN
LVHW010920110826
845149LV00013B/2433

* 9 7 8 1 0 3 2 1 8 5 9 6 5 *